CHRISTIAN GALAN ILLUSTRATED BY FLORENCE LÉROT-CALVO

I'M LEARNING
JAPANESE

LEARN TO SPEAK, READ AND WRITE THE BASICS

TUTTLE Publishing
Tokyo | Rutland, Vermont | Singapore

I'm Learning Japanese

Character Writing Practice Sheet

You may download a PDF of this writing practice sheet at www.tuttlepublishing.com

CONTENTS

5

BEFORE WE BEGIN, I HAVE TO INTRODUCE YOU TO TANUKI-SAN, WHO WILL BE MY ASSISTANT IN THIS BOOK AND WHO WILL GIVE YOU LOTS OF GOOD ADVICE...

HELLO, CHILDREN...

AND I'D LIKE EVERYONE TO INTRODUCE THEMSELVES AND SAY WHY YOU WANT TO STUDY JAPANESE.

HELLO, TANUKI-SAN. MY NAME IS EMILY, I'VE PRACTICED AIKIDO SINCE I WAS LITTLE, AND I'D LOVE TO GO TO JAPAN SOMEDAY...

I'M TÉO. I LOVE MANGA AND ANIME... AND I'M CRAZY ABOUT SUMO WRESTLING CONTESTS ON CABLE TV...

ME, I'M NICOLAS, BUT EVERYONE CALLS ME NICO. I'M FRIENDS WITH TÉO AND, UH, EMILY TOO... I MEAN, UH... I WAS JUST HANGING AROUND, I DON'T EVEN KNOW WHERE JAPAN IS... I REALLY LIKE SOCCER THOUGH... BUT THAT PROBABLY HAS NOTHING TO DO WITH THIS BOOK...

7

THE JAPANESE USE TWO SORTS OF CHARACTERS TO WRITE THEIR LANGUAGE: KANJI AND KANA. KANA (WHICH INCLUDES TWO SETS OF SYMBOLS, HIRAGANA AND KATAKANA) ARE THE CHARACTERS USED TO TRANSCRIBE SYLLABLES: A, I, U, E, O... KA, KI, KU, KE, KO... SA, SHI, SU, SE, SO... THERE ARE 46 HIRAGANA CHARACTERS IN ALL, AS YOU CAN SEE IN THE CHART BELOW.

THE CHART STARTS HERE, WITH THE SYLLABLE A; FIRST THE FIRST COLUMN, THEN THE SECOND, AND SO ON.

-N	WA	RA	YA	MA	HA/WA	NA	TA	SA	KA	A
ん	わ	ら	や	ま	は	な	た	さ	か	あ
		RI		MI	HI	NI	CHI	SHI	KI	I
		り		み	ひ	に	ち	し	き	い
		RU	YU	MU	FU	NU	TSU	SU	KU	U
		る	ゆ	む	ふ	ぬ	つ	す	く	う
		RE		ME	HE	NE	TE	SE	KE	E
		れ		め	へ	ね	て	せ	け	え
	O	RO	YO	MO	HO	NO	TO	SO	KO	O
	を	ろ	よ	も	ほ	の	と	そ	こ	お

AS FOR THE *KANJI*, THEY ARE CHARACTERS THAT CAN EACH HAVE SEVERAL READINGS AND SEVERAL MEANINGS. UNLIKE *HIRAGANA*, THERE ARE SEVERAL.... THOUSAND!!! THE JAPANESE USE *HIRAGANA* AND *KANJI* SIDE BY SIDE AND IN A COMPLEMENTARY WAY.

MOUNTAIN, WHICH CAN BE READ *YAMA*, CAN BE WRITTEN

やま
YA MA

IN *HIRAGANA* AND

山

IN *KANJI*.

RIVER, WHICH IS SAID *KAWA*, CAN BE WRITTEN

かわ
KA WA

IN *HIRAGANA* AND

川

IN *KANJI*.

AAGH!! SEVERAL THOUSAND *KANJI*...! FORGET IT. SIR FOX, CAN WE LEAVE THIS BOOK, RIGHT NOW?

YIKES! 46 CHARACTERS? THAT'S ALMOST TWICE AS MANY LETTERS AS OUR ALPHABET!

NOBODY LEAVES... DON'T PANIC! WE'LL PROCEED JUST LIKE THE YOUNG PEOPLE IN JAPAN DO TO LEARN TO READ AND WRITE. FIRST, WE'LL LEARN *HIRAGANA* AND THEN, LITTLE BY LITTLE, *KANJI*. ANYWAY, YOU'LL SEE, *HIRAGANA* ARE GREAT CHARACTERS SINCE NOT ONLY DO THEY ALLOW US TO WRITE ALL THE WORDS OF THE JAPANESE LANGUAGE, BUT ALSO, ONCE YOU HAVE LEARNED THEM, YOU'LL BE ABLE TO USE THEM EASILY BECAUSE EACH CHARACTER CORRESPONDS TO ONLY ONE SYLLABLE. AND, THE REVERSE ALSO: EACH SYLLABLE IS ALWAYS WRITTEN WITH THE SAME *HIRAGANA*. IN COMPARISON, THINK ABOUT HOW MANY WAYS THERE ARE TO WRITE DOWN THE SOUND "O" IN ENGLISH!

O, OW, OE, OA, OH, OUGH...

SLOW DOWN, I CAN'T WRITE THAT FAST...

BUT WHY'RE YOU WRITING IT DOWN, IT'S ALL PRINTED ON THE PAGE, FOOL!

FOOL?

WHILE WE DISCOVER HIRAGANA, WE'LL ALSO BEGIN TO SEE HOW JAPANESE SENTENCES WORK, AND I'M NOT GOING TO LIE TO YOU— THEY DON'T WORK AT ALL LIKE IN ENGLISH!

I WANNA GO! DON'T FEEL WELL NOW... TUMMY ACHE... SIR, SIR, CAN I GO PEE?

SENTENCES WORK BACKWARDS.

WHAT DO YOU EXPECT, JAPAN IS ON THE OTHER SIDE OF THE WORLD. THEIR HEADS ARE UPSIDE DOWN...

TSK, TSK... NOT AT ALL, NICO. JAPAN IS CERTAINLY VERY FAR AWAY FROM AMERICA, BUT IN THE SAME HEMISPHERE... SO THEY DON'T AT ALL HAVE "THEIR HEADS UPSIDE DOWN"...

I THINK IT IS URGENT, BEFORE WE GO ANY FURTHER, TO CLARIFY FOR NICO WHERE JAPAN IS, AND TO GIVE HIM SOME FACTS ABOUT MY COUNTRY.

JAPAN IS LOCATED IN FAR EAST ASIA, MEANING AT THE EXTREME EASTERN END OF THE ASIAN CONTINENT. JAPAN IS ALSO CALLED THE "LAND OF THE RISING SUN," WHICH IS REPRESENTED ON THE JAPANESE FLAG.

JAPAN IS MADE UP OF THOUSANDS OF ISLANDS: IT'S WHAT WE CALL AN ARCHIPELAGO. THE FOUR MAIN ISLANDS ARE HOKKAIDO, HONSHU, SHIKOKU AND KYUSHU. THE CAPITAL CITY IS TOKYO. THE HIGHEST MOUNTAIN IS MOUNT FUJI (FUJISAN), 12,388 FEET (3776 METERS) HIGH. THERE ARE AROUND 127 MILLION INHABITANTS, LESS THAN HALF AS MANY AS IN THE UNITED STATES.

TO GET BACK TO OUR SUBJECT, LET'S TAKE FOR EXAMPLE THE SENTENCE:

AH! THE CAT IS EATING A MOUSE!!!

YOU'RE FAKING! IT'S ALL ON PURPOSE!

TEACHER'S PET!

IN ENGLISH, IT'S THE PLACEMENT OF THE WORD WITHIN THE SENTENCE THAT TELLS YOU WHICH ONE OF THE WORDS IS THE SUBJECT, WHICH ONE IS THE DIRECT OBJECT, ETCETERA. IF YOU SAY FOR INSTANCE "THE MOUSE IS EATING THE CAT" IT CAN EITHER MEAN THAT WE'RE DEALING WITH A MONSTROUS MOUSE, OR WITH AN ANIMATED MOVIE... OR THAT THE SENTENCE ISN'T WORKING...

IN JAPANESE ON THE OTHER HAND, THE WORD PLACEMENT WITHIN THE SENTENCE DOESN'T MATTER, EXCEPT FOR THE VERB, WHICH IS ALWAYS AT THE END. INDEED, NOUNS ARE FOLLOWED BY LITTLE WORDS OF ONE OR TWO SYLLABLES, CALLED PARTICLES. THOSE PARTICLES ARE THE ONES THAT INDICATE THE FUNCTION OF THE NOUNS IN THE SENTENCE. IT'S AS IF YOU SAID IN ENGLISH:

CAT (SUBJECT) + MOUSE (DIRECT OBJECT) + EATING.

IN JAPANESE YOU CAN ALSO SAY, FOR THE EXACT SAME MESSAGE:

MOUSE (DIRECT OBJECT) + CAT (SUBJECT) + EATING.

THESE FUNCTIONS ARE THE SAME AS IN ENGLISH, SO YOU'LL HAVE TO REMEMBER WHATEVER GRAMMAR YOU LEARNED AT SCHOOL. WE'LL BE TALKING ABOUT SUBJECTS, VERBS, DIRECT OBJECTS, AND SO ON.

PFFF... ON TOP OF EVERYTHING ELSE, WE HAVE TO REMEMBER WHAT WE LEARNED IN SCHOOL?...!

SO, MOVING ON: AS ENCOURAGEMENT, I'VE GOT THREE PIECES OF GOOD NEWS THAT YOU'RE GOING TO WELCOME.

14

IN JAPANESE, THERE IS NO SINGULAR OR PLURAL.

SO NO NEED TO MAKE THOSE AGREE...

NOR IS THERE MASCULINE OR FEMININE...

SO NO NEED TO MAKE THOSE AGREE.

NOR ARE THERE ANY COMPLICATED VERB CONJUGATIONS OR TENSES...!!!

?

AND IT WORKS WITHOUT ANY OF THAT? I MEAN, DO THE JAPANESE MANAGE TO UNDERSTAND EACH OTHER?

SO NONE OF THAT TO LEARN...!!!

NO WAY...? FANTASTIC...! SO NO AGREEMENT MISTAKES, NO CONJUGATION MISTAKES...? SO, WELL, I'M STAYING AFTER ALL. IS IT POSSIBLE TO BECOME JAPANESE... RIGHT AWAY I MEAN...? YOU WOULDN'T HAPPEN TO KNOW THE ADDRESS OF THE JAPANESE EMBASSY BY ANY CHANCE?

YOU'RE SUCH A PAIN, TÉO! OF COURSE IT WORKS... THINK ABOUT IT: HAVEN'T YOU SEEN ALL THE PRODUCTS THE JAPANESE MANAGE TO MAKE? DO YOU REALLY THINK THEY DO IT ALL WITHOUT TALKING?

15

DEAR READER, YOU WHO WILL LEARN JAPANESE WITH EMILY, TÉO AND NICO AT YOUR SIDE THANKS TO THIS BOOK: GRAB A PENCIL LIKE THEM, SOME SHEETS OF PAPER...AND AN ERASER (IT IS INDEED BETTER TO ERASE A BADLY WRITTEN CHARACTER THAN TO TRY TO FIX IT).

ALL THE CHARACTERS YOU'RE GOING TO STUDY, WHATEVER NUMBER OF STROKES THEY'RE MADE OF, HAVE TO OCCUPY THE SAME SPACE ON THE PAGE. WE SAY THAT THEY ARE CONTAINED IN THE SAME "IMAGINARY" SQUARE. WE SAY "IMAGINARY" BECAUSE, MOST OF THE TIME, THE PAGES HAVE NO GRID PATTERN ACTUALLY SHOWING.

THE VARIOUS STROKES NEED, THEN, TO BE ENLARGED OR REDUCED ACCORDING TO THE COMPLEXITY OR SIMPLICITY OF THE CHARACTER YOU'RE GOING TO WRITE—IN ORDER TO OCCUPY THE SAME AREA.

はにつをくね ← INCORRECT!

はにつをくね ← CORRECT!
HA NI TSU O KU NE

START BY WRITING ON PAPER WITH A LARGE GRID PATTERN. AT THE START OF THIS BOOK, ON PAGE 2, YOU'LL FIND A GRID PATTERN THAT YOU CAN TRACE OR PHOTOCOPY. THEN AFTER A FEW DAYS OR WEEKS, YOU CAN START USING SMALLER SQUARES.

IN ORDER TO MEMORIZE *HIRAGANA* PERFECTLY, YOU WILL HAVE TO PRACTICE AS OFTEN AS POSSIBLE. YOU WILL HAVE TO WRITE THE NEW CHARACTERS AND GO BACK TO STUDY THOSE ALREADY LEARNED. LIKE THE JAPANESE YOUNG PEOPLE, YOU'LL HAVE TO PRACTICE MEMORIZING THE CHARACTERS BY WRITING EACH ONE OVER AND OVER.

SO, WE'LL START WITH THREE *HIRAGANA*: は (WA), に (NI) AND を (O). THEN WE'LL TRY AND MAKE UP JAPANESE SENTENCES.

WITH JUST THREE CHARACTERS?

YES.

I'M DREAMING: WITH THREE CHARACTERS WE'RE GONNA MAKE UP JAPANESE SENTENCES?

YES, WELL, ALMOST.

YOU'LL SEE.

?

ARE YOU SURE IT'S THE FOX WHO'S MAGICAL, OR IS IT JAPANESE?

ACTUALLY, HE DID SAY "ALMOST"...

SHH... COME ON... STOP TALKING... LET HIM TALK...

SO, OUR FIRST CHARACTER:

は
HA

は IS PRONOUNCED HA.
IT IS ALSO PRONOUNCED
WA, BUT ONLY IN ONE
SITUATION, AS WE'LL
QUICKLY SEE.
は IS MADE UP OF THREE
STROKES, THAT YOU NEED
TO LEARN IN ORDER...
WHICH IS THE CASE FOR
EVERY CHARACTER.

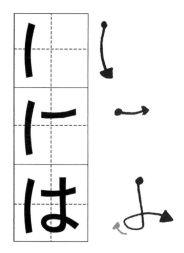

HA...

WA-F, WA-F!

に

NI

THE SECOND CHARACTER... に IS PRONOUNCED NI AND IS ALSO MADE UP OF THREE STROKES.

WITH THIS CHARACTER, WE CAN START WRITING NICO'S NAME.

19

THE THIRD CHARACTER: を IS PRONOUNCED O. AND THIS ONE ALSO IS MADE UP OF THREE STROKES.

THIS ONE'S A LITTLE BIZARRE...

AGAIN! SO... ALL THREE HAVE THREE STROKES, THEN...

WHAT, YOU DON'T FIND THE OTHER TWO BIZARRE TOO?

NOW, LET'S TRY AND MAKE JAPANESE SENTENCES WHILE RESPECTING THE RULES OF JAPANESE GRAMMAR, BUT USING ENGLISH WORDS... LET'S SPEAK "JAPANGLISH" IN A WAY...

は WA SHOWS WHAT WE'RE TALKING ABOUT (THE TOPIC OF THE SENTENCE)...

に NI SHOWS WHERE YOU ARE OR WHERE YOU ARE GOING (AMONG OTHER THINGS)...

を O SHOWS THE DIRECT OBJECT...

JAPANGLISH? HE'S COMPLETELY CRAZY, THAT FOX!

FOR INSTANCE, NICO, GIVE ME A SENTENCE, IN ENGLISH.

UM... MASTER FOX IS IN THE YARD.

WHICH GIVES US, IN JAPANESE, OR RATHER JAPANGLISH...?

WHY ALWAYS ME?

SO THAT I FORGET WHAT YOU THOUGHT VERY LOUDLY AT THE TOP OF THIS PAGE. TRY.

UH... FOX-SENSEI は (WA) YARD に (NI) TO BE.

PHEWW...

VERY GOOD.

LOOK AT THE FOLLOWING SENTENCES AND THEIR "TRANSLATIONS" IN JAPANGLISH...

Emily and Téo go to school.

Emily and Téo は (wa) school に (ni) to go.

Nico bothers Emily.

Nico は (wa) Emily を (o) to bother.

Emily slaps Nico.

Emily は (wa) Nico を (o) to slap.

COOL, I SPEAK JAPANGLISH!!

22

OK, LET'S LEARN A NEW CHARACTER... か IS PRONOUNCED KA AND IS ALSO COMPOSED OF THREE STROKES.

か IS A VERY CONVENIENT SOUND WHICH TRANSFORMS A SENTENCE INTO A QUESTION. IT'S USED LIKE A QUESTION MARK AT THE END OF THE SENTENCE BUT IT'S PRONOUNCED LIKE A SOUND.

か
KA

IN JAPANESE, QUESTIONS END WITH THE PARTICLE か AND IT IS UNNECESSARY TO ADD A QUESTION MARK.

Do Emily and Nico go to school?

Emily and Nico は (wa) school に (ni) to go か (ka).

Is Master Fox in the yard?

Fox-*sensei* は (wa) yard に (ni) to be か (ka).

OH, ALL RIGHT, ALL RIGHT...

Has Emily slapped Nico?

Emily は (wa) Nico を (o) to have slapped か (ka).

HAVE FUN TALKING AMONG YOURSELVES—AND YOU, DEAR READER, LEARN TO SPEAK JAPANGLISH TO YOUR SIBLINGS, YOUR BUDDIES, AND SURPRISE YOUR PARENTS BY SPEAKING IT AT THE TABLE FOR EXAMPLE...

BREAD は (WA) TABLE に (NI) TO BE か (KA).

YES, BREAD は (WA) TABLE に (NI) TO BE.

AFTER DINNER, WE は (WA) TV を (O) TO WATCH か (KA).

YEAH, OKAY.

CHAPTER 2: Japanese Food and Eating

NOWADAYS, JAPANESE FAMILIES EAT MORE OFTEN IN THE KITCHEN OR IN THE DINING ROOM, SEATED ON CHAIRS. BUT YOU STILL FIND MEALS SERVED TRADITIONALLY, ON LOW TABLES WITH PEOPLE SEATED ON TATAMI (MATS MADE OF RICE STRAW WHICH ARE THE TRADITIONAL FLOOR COVERING IN JAPANESE HOUSES).

The Japanese eat with chopsticks, called *hashi*, and rice is served at every meal. The Japanese eat a lot of fish, prepared in a variety of ways: broiled, marinated or . . . raw. Sliced raw fish is called sashimi, whereas raw fish on top of rice balls is called sushi.

BEFORE WE GO FURTHER, I SUGGEST A LITTLE EXERCISE: TRY TO "TRANSLATE" THE FOLLOWING SENTENCES INTO JAPANGLISH. PUT THE WORDS IN THE JAPANESE ORDER, TAKE OUT THE ARTICLES, THEN ADD THE PARTICLES は, に, を AND か. THEN TURN TO PAGE 122 TO CHECK HOW WELL YOU TRANSLATED THEM.

Do the Japanese like raw fish?

_____

Yes, the Japanese like raw fish.

Yes, _____

Where is Tanuki-san going?

_____

Tanuki-san is going into the yard.

_____

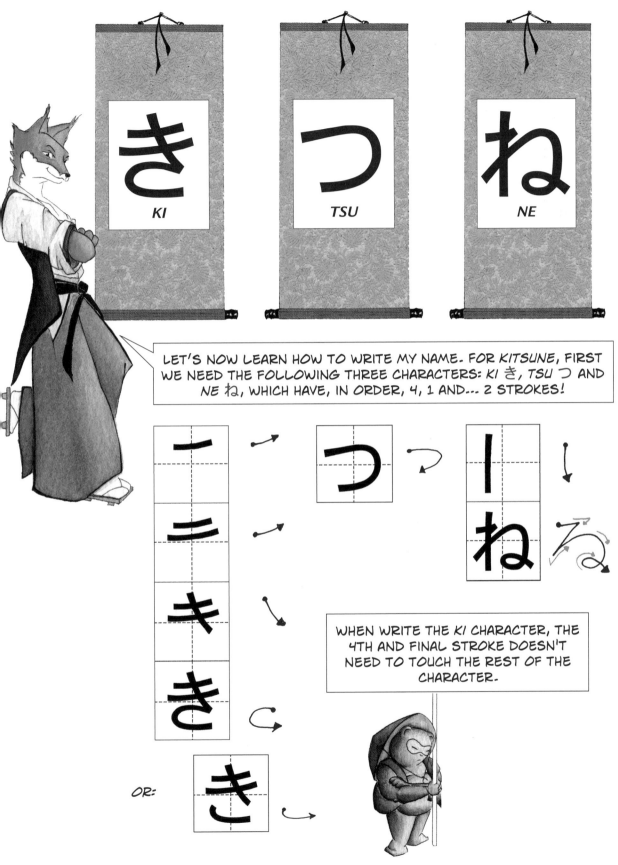

き KI

つ TSU

ね NE

LET'S NOW LEARN HOW TO WRITE MY NAME. FOR KITSUNE, FIRST WE NEED THE FOLLOWING THREE CHARACTERS: KI き, TSU つ AND NE ね, WHICH HAVE, IN ORDER, 4, 1 AND... 2 STROKES!

WHEN WRITE THE KI CHARACTER, THE 4TH AND FINAL STROKE DOESN'T NEED TO TOUCH THE REST OF THE CHARACTER.

OR:

せ
SE

ん
N

い
I

NEXT, TO WRITE SENSEI, WE NEED THE HIRAGANA SE せ, -N ん, AND I い.

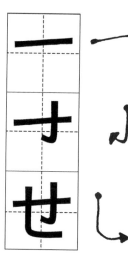

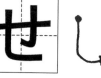

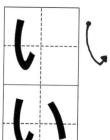

せ IS MADE UP OF THREE STROKES... PAY ATTENTION TO
THE *ORDER* OF THE STROKES.
い, ON THE OTHER HAND, IS VERY EASY TO WRITE.
ん HAS ONLY ONE STROKE: YOU HAVE TO GO DOWN TOWARD THE LEFT, THEN,
WITHOUT LIFTING YOUR PENCIL, WRITE A SORT OF BACKWARD HORIZONTAL "S".
ん IS THE ONLY *HIRAGANA* THAT IS NEVER USED BY ITSELF, BUT ALWAYS ADDED
TO ANOTHER CHARACTER:
せん *SE-N*, かん *KA-N*, にん *NI-N*, AND SO ON.

TA

NU

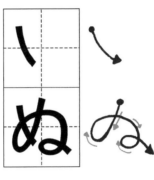

IN ORDER TO PLEASE TANUKI-SAN, LET'S NOW LEARN THE CHARACTERS USED IN HIS NAME: TA た AND NU ぬ; KI, YOU ALREADY KNOW.

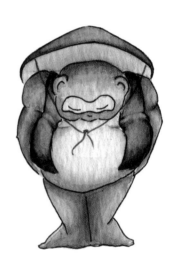

BY THE WAY, DON'T FORGET, TANUKI-SAN ASKED YOU TO WRITE EACH CHARACTER MANY TIMES TO PRACTICE WRITING THEM... AND, TO MEMORIZE THEM.

THE WORD SAN さん, WHICH FOLLOWS A FIRST NAME OR A LAST NAME, AS IN TANUKI-SAN, IS A SIGN OF RESPECT TOWARD SOMEONE. IN ENGLISH, WE TRANSLATE IT AS "MISTER," "MRS.," "MS." OR "MISS," AS THE CASE MAY BE. IN ORDER TO WRITE IT, WE NEED TO LEARN SA さ WHICH WILL BE FOLLOWED BY THE N ん YOU ALREADY LEARNED.

SA

THE RULE FOR THE ENDING OF THE CHARACTER KI き APPLIES HERE TOO: THE 3RD AND FINAL STROKE DOESN'T NEED TO TOUCH THE REST OF THE CHARACTER.

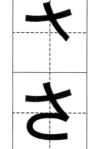

TANUKI-SAN
MR. TANUKI

TANUKI-SAN
MRS. TANUKI

TANUKI-SAN
MISS TANUKI

IN JAPANESE, SAN さん IS USED FOR MEN, WOMEN AND CHILDREN. VERY CONVENIENT!

NA

SHI

WA

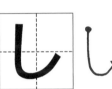

LET'S NOW STUDY THE THREE CHARACTERS NA な, SHI し AND WA わ WHICH CAN BE USED TO WRITE MANY SIMPLE WORDS AS WE'LL SEE...

わ IS WRITTEN LIKE ね, BUT WITHOUT THE LITTLE LOOP AT THE END.

-N	WA	RA	YA	MA	HA/WA	NA	TA	SA	KA	A
ん	わ	ら	や	ま	は	な	た	さ	か	あ
		RI り		MI み	HI ひ	NI に	CHI ち	SHI し	KI き	I い
		RU る	YU ゆ	MU む	FU ふ	NU ぬ	TSU つ	SU す	KU く	U う
		RE れ		ME め	HE へ	NE ね	TE て	SE せ	KE け	E え
	O を	RO ろ	YO よ	MO も	HO ほ	NO の	TO と	SO そ	KO こ	O お

BRAVO, YOU'VE ALREADY MASTERED 16 HIRAGANA OUT OF 46... THAT IS VERY GOOD. CONGRATULATIONS!

YEAH, IT'S GOOD... BUT I CAN'T TAKE IT ANYMORE! PHEW!! AND THERE ARE STILL 20 TO GO!!!

FOX-SENSEI, DO YOU THINK I'LL FIND A SHOWER IN THIS BOOK?

46 MINUS 16 EQUALS 20? GOOD JOB, TÉO... AFTER JAPANESE, DON'T FORGET TO STUDY MATH. 30. THERE ARE STILL 30 MORE...

せんせい	SENSEI	MASTER
きつね	KITSUNE	FOX
たぬきさん	TANUKI-SAN	MR. RACCOON
にわ	NIWA	YARD
かわ	KAWA	RIVER
はし	HASHI	CHOPSTICKS

WITH THESE CHARACTERS, YOU CAN NOW WRITE DOWN THE WORDS WE'VE COME ACROSS TOGETHER...

...BUT YOU CAN ALSO WRITE MANY OTHER SIMPLE WORDS... ACTUALLY, I'LL SUGGEST A LITTLE GAME: ON THE NEXT PAGE ARE SEVERAL WORDS WRITTEN WITH THE CHARACTERS WE'VE JUST LEARNED. TRY TO READ THEM, SAYING THEM OUT LOUD, AND TRY TO GUESS THEIR MEANING WITH THE HELP OF THE ILLUSTRATION. YOU CAN THEN TURN TO THE BACK OF THE BOOK TO CHECK WHETHER YOU READ THEM CORRECTLY AND GUESSED THEIR MEANINGS...

NOW YOU CAN WRITE A VERY USEFUL WORD MEANING "ME":

WATASHI わたし

I'D LOVE TO PLAY THE GAME, BUT I WOULD RATHER HAVE A SHOWER FIRST...

YEAH, GREAT, WE'RE GONNA PLAY!!! EMILY, COME QUICK...

35

HERE ARE A FEW WORDS USING SOUNDS THAT WE'VE JUST STUDIED. CAN YOU READ THEM AND UNDERSTAND THEIR MEANING WITH THE HELP OF THE DRAWINGS? YOU CAN CHECK YOUR ANSWERS BY TURNING TO PAGE 122.

はな

き

さかな

いね

いし

はた

いぬ

つき

いわ

かね

いなか

たき

はし

36

CHAPTER 3: Going to a Japanese Hot Spring

The Japanese love to take baths. At home, they take one every evening after work or school, before or after dinner. But beware, the Japanese bath is quite different from ours, because you have to wash yourself before entering the *furo* (bathtub). The bath water is very hot, and the purpose of the bath is to relax. The same water is used by all members of the family. That's why you have to be perfectly clean (and free of soap) before you enter it.

When the Japanese go on vacation, they often like to go to places where there are hot-water springs—these are called *onsen* in Japanese. There they can take a bath outdoors, day or night, even while it's snowing!

え
E

み
MI

り
RI

LET'S NOW SEE HOW TO WRITE YOUR NAMES. YOURS, EMILY, IS WRITTEN IN *HIRAGANA* WITH THREE CHARACTERS: *E* え, *MI* み AND *RI* り, EACH MADE UP OF TWO STROKES.

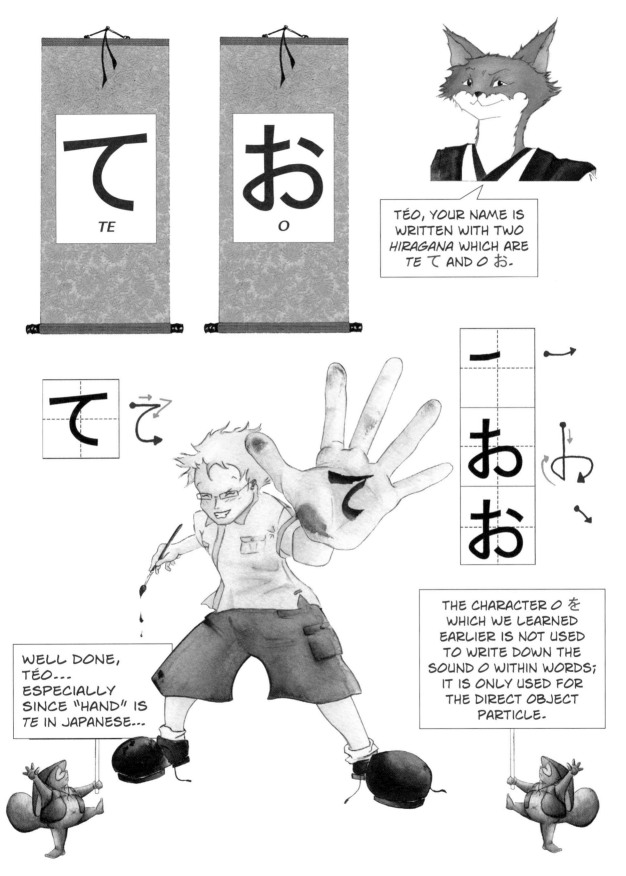

て
TE

お
O

TÉO, YOUR NAME IS WRITTEN WITH TWO *HIRAGANA* WHICH ARE TE て AND O お.

WELL DONE, TÉO... ESPECIALLY SINCE "HAND" IS TE IN JAPANESE...

THE CHARACTER O を WHICH WE LEARNED EARLIER IS NOT USED TO WRITE DOWN THE SOUND O WITHIN WORDS; IT IS ONLY USED FOR THE DIRECT OBJECT PARTICLE.

AS FOR YOU, NICOLAS, IN JAPANESE, YOUR NAME IS WRITTEN WITH THREE HIRAGANA: NI に, WHICH WE'VE ALREADY STUDIED, KO こ AND RA ら.

KO

RA

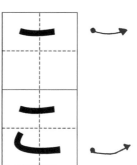

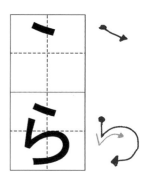

NICO, WE'LL MAKE DO WITH JUST NICO, THAT'S ENOUGH, OKAY? AND BY PRACTICING IT THIS WAY, I'LL AVOID THE BATH AGAIN, SEE... I'M TIRED OF THE INK AND THE STAINS...

あ
A

ま
MA

す
SU

LET'S NOW LOOK AT 3 NEW *HIRAGANA*... *A* あ, *MA* ま AND *SU* す. WITH THOSE, WE'LL BE ABLE TO WRITE NEW WORDS, AND MORE IMPORTANTLY, OUR FIRST TWO VERBS...

A あ AND *MA* ま HAVE 3 STROKES. MAKE SURE YOU WRITE THEM IN THE CORRECT ORDER.

SU す HAS 2 STROKES AND YOU NEED TO MAKE A LITTLE LOOP IN THE MIDDLE OF THE SECOND ONE.

43

WITH THESE NEW CHARACTERS AND THE CHARACTERS *I* い AND *RI* り THAT WE LEARNED EARLIER, WE CAN WRITE TWO VERBS THAT ARE USED QUITE OFTEN: *IMASU* います AND *ARIMASU* あります. BOTH MEAN "TO BE, TO EXIST" BUT THE FIRST IS USED FOR PEOPLE AND ANIMALS, AND THE SECOND IS USED FOR OBJECTS AND INANIMATE ITEMS.

FOR INSTANCE, WE'LL SAY:

きつね	せんせい	は	にわ	に	います。
KITSUNE	SENSEI	WA	NIWA	NI	IMASU
Fox	master		yard		to be

Master Fox is in the yard.

いぬ	は	にわ	に	います。
INU	WA	NIWA	NI	IMASU
Dog		yard		to be

The dog is in the yard.

いす	は	にわ	に	あります。
ISU	WA	NIWA	NI	ARIMASU
Chair		yard		to be

The chair is in the yard.

PLEASE NOTE: います AND ありま す ARE PRONOUNCED *IMASSS* AND *ARIMASSS*... WITHOUT MUCH EMPHASIS ON THE "U" SOUND AT THE END.

てお は みせ に います。
TÉO WA MISE NI IMASU
Téo　　　shop　　　to be

Téo is in the shop.

にこ は えき に います。
NICO WA EKI NI IMASU
Nico　　　train　　　to be
　　　　　station

Nico is in the train station.

はな は にわ に あります。
HANA WA NIWA NI ARIMASU
Flowers　　yard　　　to be
The flowers are in the yard.

いし は かわ に あります。
ISHI WA KAWA NI ARIMASU
Stones　　river　　　to be
The stones are in the river.

HAVE A GO AT READING THE FOLLOWING SENTENCES OUT LOUD, AND TRY TO UNDERSTAND THEIR MEANING. THE ILLUSTRATIONS WILL HELP YOU GUESS AT THE MEANINGS OF THE WORDS THAT WE HAVEN'T YET LEARNED. AFTERWARD, YOU CAN TURN TO PAGE 122 TO CHECK IF YOU'VE READ THEM CORRECTLY... BUT DON'T CHEAT: I'M WATCHING.

1. ねこ は にわ に います。

2. いぬ は いえ に います。

3. あり は き に います。

4. さかな は かわ に います。

5. はた は はま に あります。

6. かね は てら に あります。

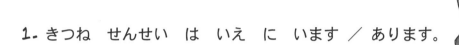

HELP NICO, TÉO AND EMILY TO FINISH THE FOLLOWING SENTENCES USING *IMASU* います OR *ARIMASU* あります. (CROSS OUT THE INCORRECT ANSWER.) MAY I REMIND YOU THAT THE WORD *IMASU* います IS FOR PEOPLE, AND THE WORD *ARIMASU* あります IS FOR THINGS. THE ANSWERS AND THE TRANSLATIONS ARE ON PAGE 122.

1. きつね せんせい は いえ に います ／ あります。

2. たき は にわ に います ／ あります。

3. たぬきさん は はま に います ／ あります。

4. てお は き に います ／ あります。

5. いわ は かわ に います ／ あります。

6. き は にわ に います ／ あります。

います ??? あります ???

PRACTICE READING THESE SENTENCES ALOUD, AND PAY ATTENTION TO PRONOUNCING IMASSS AND ARIMASSS...

I'VE ALREADY SAID THAT IN JAPANESE, THERE'S NO SINGULAR AND NO PLURAL. SO THE FOLLOWING SENTENCE:

ねこ　は　はこ　に　います。
NEKO　WA　HAKO　NI　IMASU
cat　　　　box　　　　to be

... CAN BE USED TO MEAN
EITHER
"THE CAT IS IN THE BOX"
OR
"THE CATS ARE IN THE BOX."

ねこ　は　はこ　に　います。
NEKO　WA　HAKO　NI　IMASU
The cat is in the box.

ねこ　は　はこ　に　います。
NEKO　WA　HAKO　NI　IMASU
The cats are in the box.

えみり　は　いえ　に　います。
EMILY　WA　IE　NI　IMASU
Emily is in the house.

てお　は　いえ　に　います。
TEO　WA　IE　NI　IMASU
Téo is in the house.

ARE YOU IN THE HOUSE, READER-SAN?

WE'VE ALREADY LOOKED AT TWO VERY USEFUL WORDS IN JAPANESE: IMASU います AND ARIMASU あります. THEY BOTH MEAN "IS" OR "ARE" WHEN WE TALK ABOUT THINGS THAT EXIST IN A CERTAIN PLACE. THEIR OPPOSITES ARE IMASEN いません AND ARIMASEN ありません WHICH BOTH MEAN "ISN'T" AND "AREN'T." DO YOU REMEMBER WHEN WE USE IMASU います AND WHEN WE USE ARIMASU あります? GO BACK AND CHECK ON PAGE 47 IF YOU DON'T REMEMBER.

えみり　　は　　にわ　　に　　います。
EMILY　　WA　　NIWA　　NI　　IMASU
Emily is in the yard.

えみり　　は　　にわ　　に　　いません。
EMILY　　WA　　NIWA　　NI　　IMASEN
Emily is not in the yard.

NOW THAT WE KNOW HOW TO SAY "IS" AND "ISN'T," IT'S HIGH TIME WE LEARNED TO SAY "YES" AND "NO." "YES" IS HAI はい AND "NO" IS IIE いいえ. (MAKE SURE YOU PRONOUNCE BOTH I'S: I-I-E.)

LOOK CAREFULLY NOW AT HOW QUESTIONS AND ANSWERS WORK:

いぬ　は　にわ　に　いますか。
INU　WA　NIWA　NI　IMASUKA
Is the dog in the yard?

はい、　いぬ　は　にわ　に　います。
HAI,　INU　WA　NIWA　NI　IMASU
Yes, the dog is in the yard.

HERE, EMILY COULD HAVE
ANSWERED MORE SIMPLY:
はい、います。
HAI, IMASU.
Yes, it is.

いす　は　にわ　に　ありますか。
ISU　WA　NIWA　NI　ARIMASUKA
Is the chair in the yard?

いいえ、　いす　は　にわ　に　ありません。
IIE,　ISU　WA　NIWA　NI　ARIMASEN
No, the chair is not in the yard.

TÉO COULD HAVE
SIMPLY REPLIED:
いいえ、ありません。
IIE, ARIMASEN...
No, it's not.

NOW OBSERVE THIS SCENE VERY CAREFULLY, THEN TURN THE PAGE AND ANSWER THE QUESTIONS.

FOLLOW THESE EXAMPLES AS YOU ANSWER THE QUESTIONS BELOW.
(YOU CAN CHECK YOUR ANSWERS ON PAGE 122.)

えみり　は　にわ　に　いますか。　⇨　はい、　えみり　は　にわ　に　います。
EMILY WA NIWA NI IMASUKA　　　　　　　HAI,　EMILY　WA NIWA NI　IMASU
Is Emily in the/ yard?　　　　　　　　　Yes, Emily is in the yard.
　　　　　　　　　　　　　　　　　　　(OR, MORE SIMPLY: はい、います。)

せんせい　は　にわ　に　いますか。　⇨　いいえ、せんせい　は　にわ　に　いません。
SENSEI WA NIWA NI IMASUKA　　　　　　IIE,　SENSEI　WA NIWA NI　IMASEN
Is the teacher in the yard?　　　　　　No, the teacher is not in the yard.
　　　　　　　　　　　　　　　　　　　(OR SIMPLY: いいえ、いません。)

はた　は　にわ　に　ありますか。　⇨　　　　、 _____

いす　は　にわ　に　ありますか。　⇨　　　　、 _____

はな　は　にわ　に　ありますか。　⇨　　　　、 _____

てお　は　いえ　に　いますか。　⇨　　　　、 _____

いぬ　は　かわ　に　いますか。　⇨　　　　、 _____

にこ　は　き　に　いますか。　⇨　　　　、 _____

52

LET'S SEE IF YOU REMEMBER THE WORDS WE'VE SEEN, BUT HAVEN'T USED MUCH YET. MATCH THE JAPANESE WORDS BELOW TO THE ENGLISH WORDS WITH THE SAME MEANING. (BE CAREFUL, THERE IS ONE WORD IN *HIRAGANA* THAT HAS TWO MEANINGS... CAN YOU FIND IT?) YOU'LL FIND THE ANSWERS ON PAGE 123.

1. はし ・

2. えき ・

3. いぬ ・

4. みせ ・

5. はま ・

6. つき ・

7. いなか・

・ A. COUNTRYSIDE

・ B. STORE

・ C. MOON

・ D. CHOPSTICKS

・ E. TRAIN STATION

・ F. DOG

・ G. BEACH

・ H. BRIDGE

TRY TO READ THE TWO WORDS BELOW OUT LOUD AND FIGURE OUT THE MEANING. THESE WORDS COME FROM JAPANESE BUT ARE NOW COMMONLY USED IN ENGLISH.

SINCE YOU'VE WORKED HARD, I SUGGEST WE NOW TAKE A BREAK IN CERTAIN QUIET AND BEAUTIFUL PLACES THAT YOU FIND ACROSS JAPAN: A *SHINTO* SHRINE AND A BUDDHIST MONASTERY.

A. つなみ _____

B. からて _____

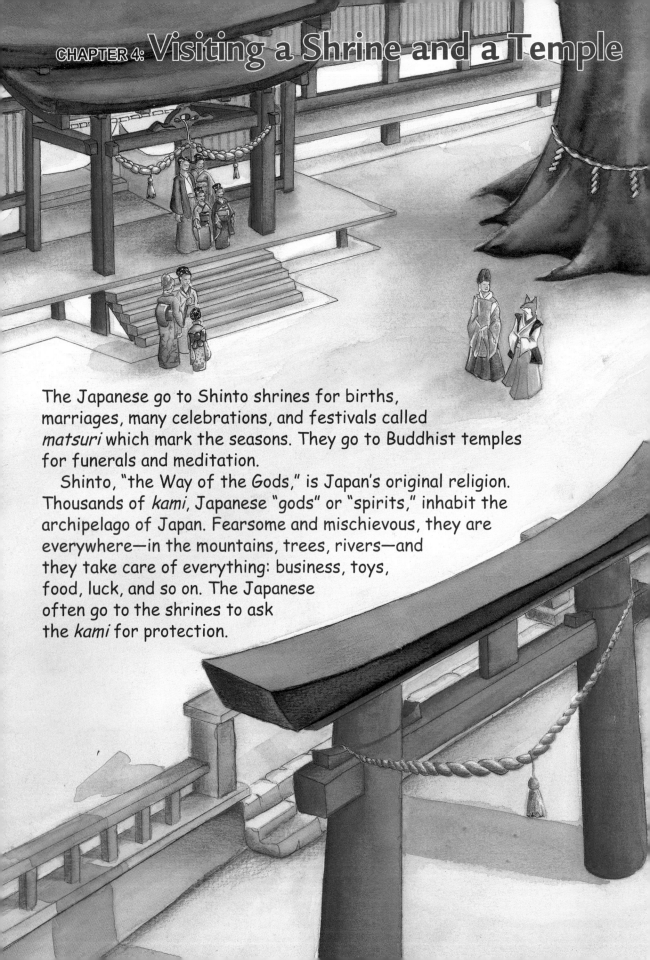

CHAPTER 4: Visiting a Shrine and a Temple

The Japanese go to Shinto shrines for births, marriages, many celebrations, and festivals called *matsuri* which mark the seasons. They go to Buddhist temples for funerals and meditation.

Shinto, "the Way of the Gods," is Japan's original religion. Thousands of *kami*, Japanese "gods" or "spirits," inhabit the archipelago of Japan. Fearsome and mischievous, they are everywhere—in the mountains, trees, rivers—and they take care of everything: business, toys, food, luck, and so on. The Japanese often go to the shrines to ask the *kami* for protection.

Buddhism came from India via China and spread all over Japan starting in the 5th century. Both a philosophy and a religion, Buddhism is concerned with the fate of human beings and the human condition.

In Zen Buddhism, monks practice meditation in a position called *zazen*, which means seated while cross-legged, knees on the ground, straight-backed, fingers of the left and right hand touching.

BEFORE LEARNING NEW *HIRAGANA*, I WOULD LIKE TO SHOW YOU HOW WE CAN WRITE NEW SOUNDS JUST BY ADDING LITTLE DASHES ゛ ON THE TOP RIGHT-HAND SIDE OF CERTAIN CHARACTERS THAT WE'VE ALREADY LEARNED.

FOR EXAMPLE, *KA* か ＋゛ BECOMES THE *GA* SOUND が, *KI* き ＋゛ = *GI* ぎ, AND SO ON.

KA か ＋゛ → *GA* が		*KI* き ＋゛ → *GI* ぎ
KO こ ＋゛ → *GO* ご		*SA* さ ＋゛ → *ZA* ざ
SHI し ＋゛ → *JI* じ		*SU* す ＋゛ → *ZU* ず
SE せ ＋゛ → *ZE* ぜ		*TSU* つ ＋゛ → *ZU* づ
TA た ＋゛ → *DA* だ		(NOT USED MUCH)

HEE HEE...

DON'T YOU THINK TÉO'S A LITTLE がが?

THIS ONE'S GREAT. WE'VE JUST LEARNED 11 NEW LETTERS IN ONE FELL SWOOP: COOL!!!

HERE ARE SOME WORDS USING THE SOUNDS THAT WE'VE JUST LEARNED. CAN YOU READ THEM AND UNDERSTAND THEIR MEANING WITH THE HELP OF THE DRAWINGS? YOU CAN CHECK YOUR ANSWERS BY TURNING TO PAGE 123.

たまご

はがき

まんが

でんわ

からだ

かぎ

かんじ

てがみ

えだ

かばん

でんき

ざぜん

NOW LET'S LEARN A NEW WAY TO CREATE SENTENCES. MANY JAPANESE SENTENCES ARE BUILT IN THE FOLLOWING WAY:

(something or someone) は + (description) です。

FOR INSTANCE:

わたし	は	せんせい	です。
WATASHI	*WA*	*SENSEI*	*DESU*
I	(topic)	teacher	[to be]

I am a teacher.

なまえ	は	きつね	です。
NAMAE	*WA*	*KITSUNE*	*DESU*
name	(topic)	Kitsune	[to be]

My name is Kitsune.

BE CAREFUL:
THE VERB "TO BE" IN ENGLISH HAS TWO DIFFERENT FUNCTIONS:
1. IT MEANS "TO EXIST," "TO BE (SOMEWHERE)"; AND
2. IT ENABLES A COMMENT TO BE MADE ON THE TOPIC OF THE SENTENCE: "A IS B."
IN JAPANESE TWO *DIFFERENT* WORDS ARE USED FOR THESE TWO FUNCTIONS. FOR THE FIRST ONE (TO BE, TO EXIST), WE CAN USE THE VERBS *IMASU* OR *ARIMASU*... WHEREAS FOR THE SECOND ONE, WE NEED TO USE THE WORD *DESU*.

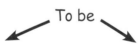

To be

to exist,
to be somewhere

↓

I am in Tokyo.
Nico is in the yard.
The chair is in the yard.

↓

IMASU います
ARIMASU あります

A is B

↓

I am Japanese.
Nico is nice.
The chair is pretty.

↓

DESU です

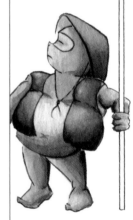

IN THE SAME WAY THAT います AND あります ARE PRONOUNCED IMASSS AND ARIMASSSS... WITHOUT THE U SOUND, AT THE END, IN EVERYDAY SPEECH... です IS PRONOUNCED DESSS, WITHOUT THE U SOUND.

THE NEGATIVE FORM OF DESU IS DE WA ARIMASEN, ではありません.

CAN YOU READ AND UNDERSTAND THE SENTENCES ON THIS PAGE? YOU CAN CHECK YOUR ANSWERS BY TURNING TO PAGE 123.

なまえ は えみり です。
いえ に いません。
おんせん に います。

わたし は にこ ではありまん。
てお です。にわ に います。

わたし は いえ に います。
なまえ は にこ です。いえ
は いなか に あります。

ほ
HO

ふ
FU

ち
CHI

LET'S LEARN THREE NEW *HIRAGANA*: HO ほ, FU ふ AND CHI ち.
WITH THE FIRST TWO WE CAN WRITE THESE WORDS:

JAPAN	NIHON	にほん
A JAPANESE MAN OR WOMAN	NIHONJIN	にほんじん
THE JAPANESE LANGUAGE	NIHONGO	にほんご
AMERICA	AMERIKA	あめりか
AN AMERICAN	AMERIKAJIN	あめりかじん
THE ENGLISH LANGUAGE	EIGO	えいご

YOU'VE GOT IT: JIN MEANS "PERSON" AND GO MEANS "LANGUAGE."

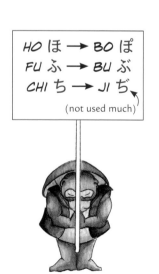

HO ほ → BO ぽ
FU ふ → BU ぶ
CHI ち → JI ぢ
(not used much)

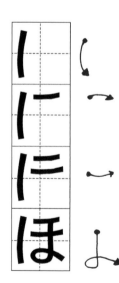

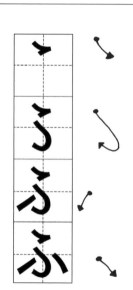

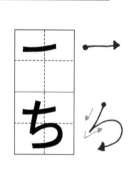

SO

RE

と

TO

THE FOLLOWING THREE HIRAGANA— SO そ, RE れ, AND TO と—WILL BE PARTICULARLY USEFUL IN LEARNING NEW EXPRESSIONS.

WHO WANTS A くき?

SO そ → ZO ぞ
TO と → DO ど

NOW THAT YOU KNOW THE LETTERS SO そ, RE れ, A あ AND KO こ, YOU CAN WRITE THE THREE IMPORTANT WORDS: KORE これ, SORE それ AND ARE あれ. IN ENGLISH THESE WORDS MEAN *THIS, THESE, THAT, THOSE.*

KORE これ INDICATES SOMETHING CLOSE TO THE PERSON SPEAKING; SORE それ INDICATES SOMETHING CLOSE TO THE PERSON SPOKEN TO; AND ARE あれ INDICATES SOMETHING THAT IS FAR FROM BOTH PEOPLE. KORE これ, SORE それ AND ARE あれ CANNOT BE USED TO REFER TO PEOPLE, ONLY TO THINGS.

あれ　は　ふじさん　です。
ARE　WA　FUJISAN　DESU
(Over there) is Mount Fuji.

それ　は　とり　です。
SORE　WA　TORI　DESU
Those are birds.

これ　は　こい　です
KORE　WA　KOI　DESU
These are carp.

A. えみり は あめりかじん [_____]。◯
EMILY WA AMERIKAJIN

B. えみり は にわ に [_____]。◯
EMILY WA NIWA NI

C. これ は さかな [_____]。◯
KORE WA SAKANA

D. さかな は こい [_____]。◯
SAKANA WA KOI

E. こい は いけ に [_____]。◯
KOI WA IKE NI

F. き は にわ に [_____]。◯
KI WA NIWA NI

G. いす は いえ に [_____]。◯
ISU WA IE NI

H. これ は ねこ [_____]。◯
KORE WA NEKO

I. きつね せんせい は にほん に [_____]。◯
KITSUNE SENSEI WA NIHON NI

J. ふじさん は にほん に [_____]。◯
FUJISAN WA NIHON NI

1. THIS IS A CAT.
2. THE TREES ARE IN THE YARD.
3. MASTER KITSUNE IS IN JAPAN.
4. THE CHAIR IS IN THE HOUSE.
5. MOUNT FUJI IS IN JAPAN.
6. EMILY IS AMERICAN.
7. THE CARP ARE IN THE POND.
8. THESE ARE FISH.
9. THE FISH ARE CARP.
10. EMILY IS IN THE YARD.

HELP EMILY, NICO AND TÉO COMPLETE THESE SENTENCES USING DESU です, IMASU います OR ARIMASU あります. THEN WRITE IN THE CIRCLE THE NUMBER OF THE MATCHING ENGLISH MEANING BELOW. CHECK YOUR ANSWERS ON PAGE 123.

です？
います？
あります？

BE CAREFUL WITH THE PRONUNCIATION OF THE WORD KOI こい (CARP): YOU HAVE TO SEPARATE BOTH OF THE VOWELS O-I AND SAY KO-I. (NOT LIKE THE ENGLISH WORD "COY.")

LET'S NOW LEARN SOME SHORT, AND VERY SIMPLE, WORDS WITH WHICH YOU ASK QUESTIONS.

1. NANI なに (OR NAN なん IN FRONT OF CERTAIN SOUNDS—T, D, N) ASKS ABOUT THE NATURE OF THINGS: WHAT?
2. DOKO どこ ASKS ABOUT PLACE: WHERE?
3. DARE だれ ASKS ABOUT PEOPLE: WHO?

1

なに	OR	なん
NANI		NAN

なん　ですか。
NAN　DESUKA
What is this?

はな　です。

2

どこ
DOKO

たぬきさん　は　どこ　に　いますか。
TANUKI-SAN WA DOKO NI IMASUKA
Where is Tanuki-san?

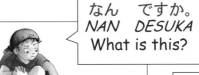

いえ　に　います。

3

だれ
DARE

だれ　ですか
DARE　DESUKA
Who is it?

たぬきさん　です。

CAN YOU READ AND UNDERSTAND WHAT'S IN THESE BOXES AND MATCH THEM TO THE DRAWINGS BELOW? YOU'LL FIND THE ANSWERS ON PAGE 123.

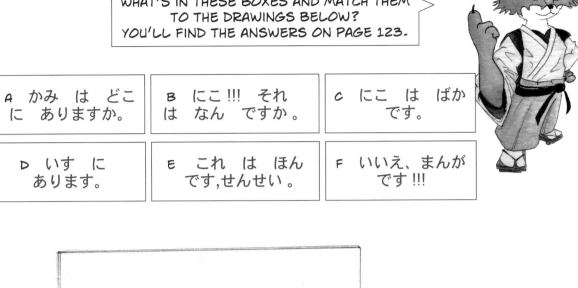

A かみ は どこ に ありますか。

B にこ !!! それ は なん ですか。

C にこ は ばか です。

D いす に あります。

E これ は ほん です,せんせい。

F いいえ、まんが です !!!

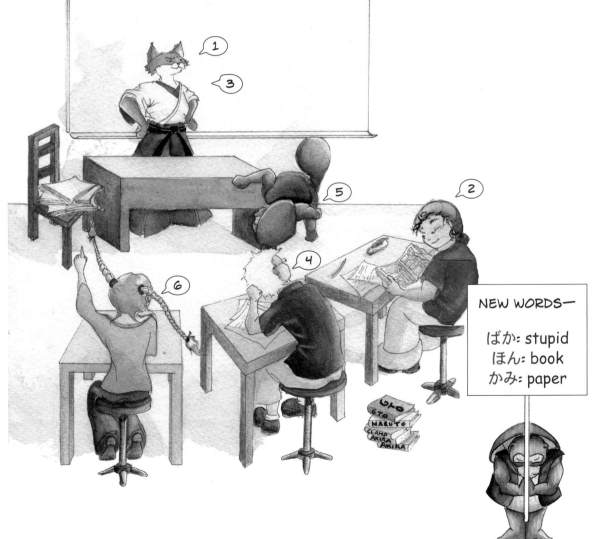

NEW WORDS—

ばか: stupid
ほん: book
かみ: paper

TO LINK TWO NOUNS TOGETHER (NOUNS OR PROPER NOUNS) IN JAPANESE THE WAY "AND" DOES IN ENGLISH, YOU USE THE PARTICLE TO と.

SO IN ORDER TO SAY: EMILY AND NICO
YOU SAY: EMILY と NICO ➡ えみり と にこ

CAN YOU READ AND UNDERSTAND THIS CONVERSATION BELOW BETWEEN EMILY AND TÉO?

えみり：　せんせい　と　たぬきさん　は　にわ
　　　　　に　いますか。

てお：　　いいえ、いません。いえ　に　います。

えみり：　これ　は　なん　ですか。

てお：　　それ　は　ほん　と　まんが　です。

てお：　　それ　は　なん　ですか。

えみり：　てがみ　と　はがき　です。

YOU CAN FIND THE ENGLISH TRANSLATION ON PAGE 123.

SENSEI... HOW DO YOU SAY "I AM TIRED" IN JAPANESE?

YOU SAY: つかれました TSUKAREMASHITA.

OKAY, HERE WE GO: つかれました, せんせい!!

OKAY, OKAY. I SUGGEST WE LOOK AT THREE MORE VERY, VERY SIMPLE CHARACTERS, KU く, HE へ, AND U う, THEN WE TAKE A BREAK... AND I WILL TAKE YOU TO SEE SOME SPORTS EVENTS THE JAPANESE LOVE.

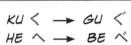

KU く → GU ぐ
HE へ → BE べ

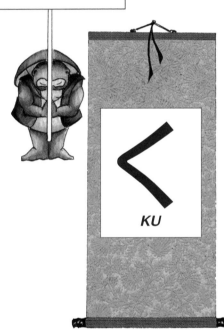

く

KU

へ

HE

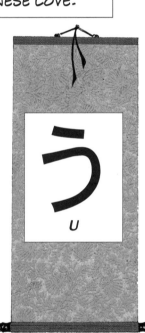

う

U

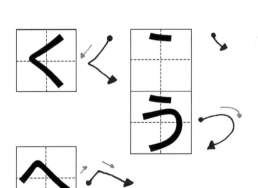

GREAT...AND HOW DO YOU SAY "THANK YOU" IN JAPANESE?

YOU SAY ありがとう, PRONOUNCED AH-RI-GA-TO-O...

THEN: ありがとう, せんせい!!

CHAPTER 5: Sports in Japan

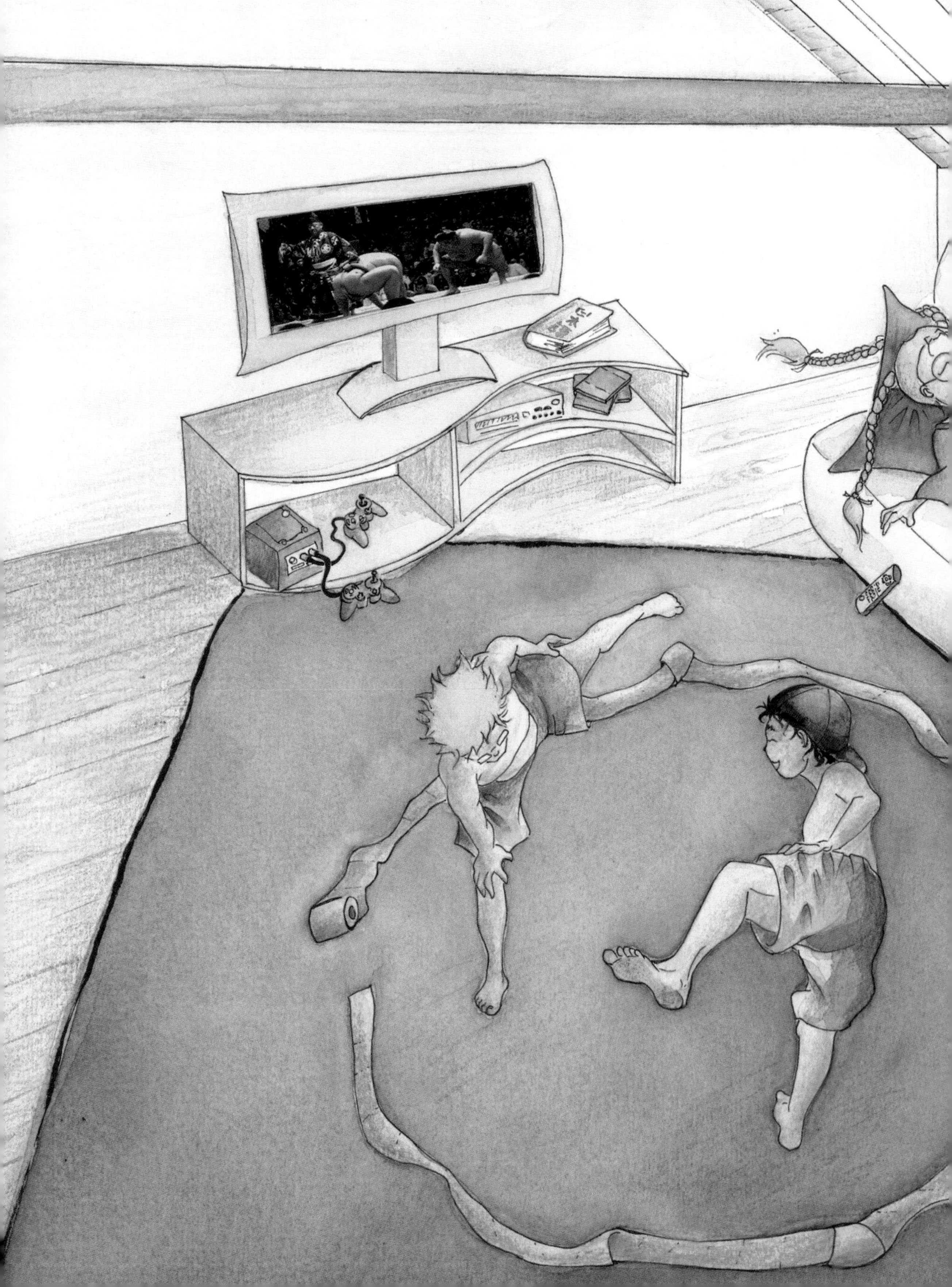

Sumo is an ancient fighting style where two wrestlers called *rikishi* oppose each other. They're usually very large (many weigh more than 300 pounds, and sometimes 400 pounds, which doesn't prevent them from being very agile). The goal is to force the opponent to step out of the 15-foot ring drawn on the clay arena (ouch!! the falls!) or to make him touch the ground with any part of his body... except the soles of his feet, naturally. There are six big tournaments held each year, and the highest rank that a sumo champion can attain is *yokozuna*.

THE JAPANESE REALLY LOVE SPORTS. THEIR FAVORITE SPORTS ARE BASEBALL AND SUMO. IN ENGLISH, WE WRITE SUMO, BUT IN JAPANESE, IN HIRAGANA, IT'S すもう AND IS PRONOUNCED SUMO-O AS IF THERE WERE TWO O'S AT THE END. BASEBALL WAS IMPORTED FROM THE UNITED STATES AT THE END OF THE NINETEENTH CENTURY, AND THE JAPANESE IMMEDIATELY ADOPTED IT. THE OLDEST AND MOST FAMOUS PRO BASEBALL TEAM IS THE TOKYO GIANTS.

| To eat: | たべます | にこ は すし を たべます。 |
| | TABEMASU | |

To eat: たべます
TABEMASU

にこ は すし を たべます。

To do: します
SHIMASU

えみり は なに を しますか。

To buy: かいます
KAIMASU

てお は まんが を かいます。

To learn: ならいます
NARAIMASU

わたし は にほんご を ならいます。

To look at: みます
MIMASU

きつね せんせい は ふじさん を みます。

To write: かきます
KAKIMASU

にこ は てがみ を かきます。

To listen: ききます
KIKIMASU

えみり は うた を ききます。

AS WE SAW AT THE BEGINNING OF THIS BOOK, THE を PARTICLE INDICATES A DIRECT OBJECT FOR VERBS. THESE VERBS WORK JUST LIKE IN ENGLISH.

ABOVE ARE SOME VERY COMMON VERBS THAT ARE VERY EASY TO USE. TRY TO READ AND UNDERSTAND THE SENTENCES. THEN YOU CAN TURN TO PAGE 124 TO CHECK HOW YOU DID.

LET'S NOW TAKE A LOOK AT THE *HIRAGANA* FOR THE *NO* SOUND: の

NO

USING THIS CHARACTER, WE CAN INDICATE A RELATIONSHIP BETWEEN NOUNS, JUST LIKE 'S IN ENGLISH. IN JAPANESE, THE "OWNING" NOUN GOES BEFORE THE "OWNED" NOUN, LIKE IN ENGLISH. SO THE THING THAT IS OWNED ALWAYS COMES LAST. FOR EXAMPLE, TO SAY:

Emily's cat...

we'll say:　Emily の cat...　　えみり　の　ねこ…
　　　　　　　　　　　　　　　　EMIRI　NO　NEKO

To say:　　Tanuki-san's yard's flowers...

We'll say:　Tanuki-san の yard の flowers...

たぬきさん　の　にわ　の　はな…
TANUKI-SAN NO NIWA NO　HANA...

IN ENGLISH, SOMETIMES YOU MIGHT SAY IT THE OPPOSITE WAY—FOR EXAMPLE, YOU MIGHT SAY "THE HOUSE OF THE TEACHER." BUT IN JAPANESE, THAT'S COMPLETELY IMPOSSIBLE. YOU MUST SAY "THE TEACHER'S HOUSE" WITH THE WORDS IN THAT ORDER.

teacher の house...　　せんせい　の　いえ…
NO　　　　　　　　　SENSEI　NO　IE

"Boy" for instance is said おとこ　の　こ and is made up of two words linked by の.

OTOKO　NO　KO
male　　's　child

So a boy is a "male child."

The following words have the same construction:

おんな　　の　　こ
ONNA　　NO　　KO
female　　's　　child

= a (small) girl or young girl

おとこ　の　　ひと
OTOKO　NO　　HITO
male　　's　　person

= a man

おんな　　の　　ひと
ONNA　　NO　　HITO
woman　　's　person

= a woman

In the same way, you say "my," "your" like this in Japanese:

わたし　の　ほん
WATASHI　NO　HON
I　　's　book

= my book

あなた　の　　ほん
ANATA　NO　　HON
you　　's　　book

= your book

あなた　　の　　はし
ANATA　　NO　　HASHI
you　　　's　chopsticks

= your chopsticks

We find the same principle in words like:

にほんじん
NIHONJIN
NIHON + JIN

= Japan + person
= a Japanese man or woman

にほんご
NIHONGO
NIHON + GO

= Japan + language
= the Japanese language

ふじさん
FUJISAN
FUJI + SAN

= Fuji + mountain
= Mount Fuji

SO EMILY, PLEASE SUGGEST A SENTENCE SO TÉO CAN TRANSLATE IT INTO JAPANGLISH; THEN TÉO CAN SUGGEST A SENTENCE FOR NICO TO TRANSLATE. THEN, NICO WILL SUGGEST A SENTENCE AND EMILY WILL TRANSLATE IT... GO AHEAD, I'M WATCHING...

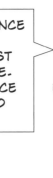

MAKIKO'S DOG IS IN THE TEACHER'S YARD.

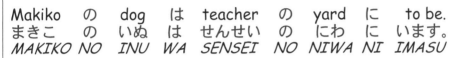

Makiko	の	dog	は	teacher	の	yard	に	to be.
まきこ	の	いぬ	は	せんせい	の	にわ	に	います。
MAKIKO	*NO*	*INU*	*WA*	*SENSEI*	*NO*	*NIWA*	*NI*	*IMASU*

TANUKI-SAN'S COUSIN IS IN THE FLOWER SHOP.

Tanuki-san	の	cousin	は	flower	の	shop	に	to be.
たぬきさん	の	いとこ	は	はな	の	みせ	に	います。
TANUKI-SAN	*NO*	*ITOKO*	*WA*	*HANA*	*NO*	*MISE*	*NI*	*IMASU*

THIS IS MAKIKO'S KARATE TEACHER'S COUSIN'S SCHOOLBAG.

HOW CLEVER!

This	は	Makiko	の	karate	の	teacher	の	cousin	の	schoolbag	to be.
これ	は	まきこ	の	からて	の	せんせい	の	いとこ	の	かばん	です。
KORE	*WA*	*MAKIKO*	*NO*	*KARATE*	*NO*	*SENSEI*	*NO*	*ITOKO*	*NO*	*KABAN*	*DESU.*

NEW WORDS...

まきこ: Makiko (girl's name)
いとこ: cousin

VERY GOOD, GUYS... ESPECIALLY EMILY. NICO, SINCE YOU LIKE TO PLAY, HERE'S A LITTLE EXERCISE JUST FOR YOU... TRY TO PLACE THE PARTICLES は, に, と, を, の AS NEEDED. THEN YOU CAN TURN TO PAGE 124 TO CHECK WHETHER YOU'VE DONE IT RIGHT. ALSO TRANSLATE THE SENTENCES BELOW...

これ＿＿＿＿＿わたし＿＿＿＿＿かばん　です。

きつねせんせい＿＿＿＿＿たぬきさん＿＿＿＿＿にわ＿＿＿＿＿います。

にこ＿＿＿＿＿てお＿＿＿＿＿あめりかじん　です。

てお＿＿＿＿＿ほん＿＿＿＿＿まんが＿＿＿＿＿かいます。

わたし＿＿＿＿＿いえ＿＿＿＿＿いなか＿＿＿＿＿あります。

えみり＿＿＿＿＿はし＿＿＿＿＿これ　です。

にこ＿＿＿＿＿うた＿＿＿＿＿ききます。

AS I TOLD YOU AT THE BEGINNING OF THIS BOOK, THE は PARTICLE (READ WA) IS USED TO INDICATE THE TOPIC OF A SENTENCE, TELLING WHAT THE OVERALL SENTENCE IS ABOUT. I'VE ALSO TOLD YOU THAT MANY JAPANESE SENTENCES START LIKE THIS, WITH AN INDICATION OF THE TOPIC USING は. I NOW HAVE TO COMPLETE MY EXPLANATION: WHAT WE CALL "TOPIC" IS SOMETHING THAT HAS BEEN TALKED ABOUT ALREADY (OR SOMETHING KNOWN BY THE PEOPLE TALKING, EITHER BECAUSE IT IS IN FRONT OF THEM, OR BECAUSE ONE SHOWS IT TO THE OTHER) AND SOME FACTS ARE GIVEN ABOUT IT. BUT ON THE OTHER HAND, IF A VERB'S SUBJECT HAS NOT YET BEEN INTRODUCED AND IT IS BEING PRESENTED FOR THE FIRST TIME, THEN THE PARTICLE は WILL NOT BE USED AND INSTEAD が (GA) WILL BE USED. LOOK AT THE EXAMPLES BELOW.

ああ、にわ に ねこ が います。

ねこ は もも です。 わたし の ねこ です。

Nico, who sees the cat for the first time, says:

ああ、	にわ	に	ねこ	が	います。
AA,	NIWA	NI	NEKO	GA	IMASU.
Ah!	yard	(place)	cat	(topic)	to be

Ah, A cat is in the yard.
Ah, there is A cat in the yard.

Master Fox, who knows the cat in question, says:

ねこ	は	もも	です。	わたし	の	ねこ	です。
NEKO	WA	MOMO	DESU	WATASHI	NO	NEKO	DESU
Cat	(topic)	Momo	to be	I	(describing)	cat	to be

THE cat (you're talking about) is named Momo. It's my cat.

THE "TOPIC" FUNCTION DOESN'T REALLY EXIST IN ENGLISH IN THE SAME WAY, BUT IT CAN BE APPROXIMATED BY USING THE PHRASE "AS FOR"... AT THE BEGINNING OF A SENTENCE.

As for Emily, she is in the yard.
(topic)

In English, in this type of sentence, we repeat the topic (with the pronoun—"she" in this case) before stating its relation to the rest of the sentence.

Whereas in Japanese, this is not necessary:

えみり　　は　　にわ　　に　　います。
EMILY　　WA　　NIWA　　NI　　IMASU
Emily　　(topic)　　yard　　(place)　　to be.
As for Emily, she is in the yard.
= Emily is in the yard.

In almost all the sentences we've seen, the topic of the sentence is also the subject of the verb. That's because you're just starting to learn Japanese, and these sentences are very simple. But a topic can also have different functions. For instance, a direct object can come right after it as in the example below. Everything depends on what the speaker wants to emphasize:

えみり　　は　　おかし　　　　を　　　　たべます。
EMILY　　WA　　OKASHI　　　　O　　　　TABEMASU
Emily　　(topic)　　cakes　　(direct object)　　to eat.
As for Emily, she is eating cakes.

おかし　　は　　えみり　　　　が　　　　たべます。
OKASHI　　WA　　EMILY　　　　GA　　　　TABEMASU
Cakes　　(topic)　　Emily　　(subject)　　to eat.
As for the cakes, Emily eats them. = The cakes, it's Emily who's eating them.

TO SIMPLIFY ALL THIS, WE CAN SAY THAT THE TOPIC は (WA) INDICATES THE "MAIN SUBJECT" OF THE WHOLE SENTENCE, WHAT IT IS ABOUT AS A WHOLE, WHEREAS が (GA) CLARIFIES WHICH SUBJECT, OFTEN SOMETHING NOT NAMED BEFORE.
AND EACH TIME A QUESTION WORD APPEARS IN A SENTENCE AS SUBJECT, IT IS ALWAYS FOLLOWED BY が SINCE IT ASKS ABOUT SOMETHING THAT'S NOT KNOWN. AND, TO ANSWER, THE SAME WORD IS USED. CAN YOU COMPLETE THE DIALOGUES BELOW BETWEEN EMILY AND TÉO USING は OR が? YOU'LL FIND THE ANSWERS AND THE TRANSLATED SENTENCES ON PAGE 125.

1. えみり： いす　に　なに　＿＿＿　ありますか。

2. てお：　 まんが　＿＿＿　あります。

3. えみり： まんが　＿＿＿　だれ　の　まんが　ですか。

4. てお：　 わたし　の　まんが　です。

5. えみり： これ　＿＿＿　なん　ですか。　まんが　ですか。

6. てお：　 いいえ、これ　＿＿＿　にほんご　の　ほん　です。

7. えみり： にわ　に　さくら＿＿＿　ありますか。

8. てお：　 はい、あります。

THAT'S NOT FAIR! THEY CAN HAVE MANGA AND NOBODY SAYS ANYTHING!!!

UNLIKE IN ENGLISH, WHERE IT'S IMPOSSIBLE TO MAKE A SENTENCE WITHOUT A SUBJECT, IN JAPANESE, IT'S NOT NECESSARY TO REPEAT THE TOPIC (OR SUBJECT) IF IT IS CLEAR FROM THE CONTEXT. SO IN THE LAST SENTENCE OF THE PRECEDING PAGE, TÉO ANSWERS: はい、あります。 (YES, TO BE) RATHER THAN SAYING: "YES, THERE IS A CHERRY TREE" OR "YES, THERE IS."

Similarly, to the question:

これ	は	ほん	ですか。
KORE	WA	HON	DESUKA
This	(topic)	book	[to be]?

Is this a book?

You can answer very naturally, without repeating これ は, "this:"

はい、	ほん	です。
HAI	HON	DESU
Yes,	book	[to be].

Yes, this is a book.

Finally, to say: "Nico is an American. He studies Japanese," we can simply say:

にこ	は	あめりかじん	です。	にほんご	を	ならいます。
NICO	WA	AMERIKAJIN	DESU	NIHONGO	O	NARAIMASU
Nico	(topic)	American	[to be].	Japanese	(direct object)	to study.

...without needing to say "he" in the second sentence.

IN THE SAME WAY, WHEN THE TOPIC IS "I" OR "YOU," THE WORDS WATASHI WA, わたし は AND ANATA WA, あなた は ARE RARELY SAID. IN BOTH CASES, THE TOPIC IS USUALLY OBVIOUS, SO THE JAPANESE DON'T BOTHER USING THESE WORDS.

(あなた は)	てがみ	を	かきますか。
(ANATA WA)	TEGAMI	O	KAKIMASUKA?
(You topic)	letter	(direct object)	to write?

You're writing a letter?

はい、	(わたし は)	かきます。
HAI,	(WATASHI WA)	KAKIMASU.
Yes	(me topic)	to write.

Yes, I am.

WELL, WELL, WELL...LOOK, GUYS, OUR HIRAGANA CHART IS ALMOST COMPLETE...

ARE YOU ABLE TO COMPLETE THE CHART FILLING IN ALL THE CHARACTERS WE'VE LEARNED, WITHOUT LOOKING BACK AT THE PREVIOUS PAGES?

-N	WA	RA	YA	MA	HA/WA	NA	TA	SA	KA	A
		RI		MI	HI ひ	NI	CHI	SHI	KI	I
		RU る	YU ゆ	MU む	FU	NU	TSU	SU	KU	U
		RE		ME め	HE	NE	TE	SE	KE け	E
	O	RO ろ	YO よ	MO も	HO	NO	TO	SO	KO	O

SINCE WE'RE ONLY MISSING TEN CHARACTERS NOW... I SUGGEST WE LEARN THEM RIGHT AWAY, TO BE DONE WITH IT!!!

I WILL ALSO INTRODUCE SOME NEW WORDS AND SEVERAL VERY SIMPLE SENTENCE STRUCTURES WHICH YOU CAN USE TO SAY LOTS OF THINGS...

KE

HI

MU

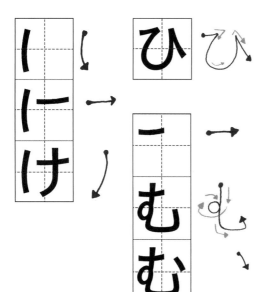

THERE ARE NO PROBLEMS WITH THE THREE *HIRAGANA* KE け, HI ひ AND MU む. BUT MAKE SURE YOU WRITE THE LOOP OF THE む CHARACTER CAREFULLY, FOLLOWING THE MODEL. BY THE WAY, I HAVEN'T ASKED YOU IN A LONG TIME, BUT I ASSUME YOU'RE STILL PRACTICING WRITING EACH CHARACTER MANY TIMES, RIGHT...? ALL RIGHT, I BELIEVE YOU.

KE け → GE げ
HI ひ → BI び

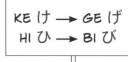

80

WE'VE ALREADY SEEN THAT THE PARTICLE *NI* に, USED WITH "STAY" VERBS (TO BE, TO STAY, TO LIVE, ETC.) AND PLACED AFTER A PLACE NAME, INDICATES WHERE ONE IS, STAYS OR LIVES, ETC. THE SAME GOES FOR "MOVEMENT" VERBS (TO GO, TO COME, TO ENTER, TO COME BACK, ETC.): IT INDICATES THE PLACE WHERE ONE GOES, COMES, ETC. LOOK CLOSELY AT THESE EXAMPLES; THERE ARE NEW VERBS TO STUDY:

えみり　は　うみ　に　いきます。
EMILY　WA　UMI　NI　IKIMASU
　　　　　　SEA　　　TO GO

Emily goes to the sea.

てお　は　いえ　に　はいります。
TÉO　WA　IE　NI　HAIRIMASU
　　　　　　　　　TO ENTER

Téo enters into the house.

However, when an <u>action</u> is to occur, another particle is instead of *ni* に — the particle *de* で. For instance, to say "Téo is in the yard," we use に:

てお　は　にわ　に　います。
TÉO　WA　NIWA　NI　IMASU

And to say "Téo goes into the yard," we'll still use に:

てお　は　にわ　に　いきます。
TÉO　WA　NIWA　NI　IKIMASU

But to say "Téo <u>writes a letter</u> in the yard," we use で instead:

てお　は　にわ　で　てがみ　を　かきます。
TÉO　WA　NIWA　DE　TEGAMI　O　KAKIMASU

In the same way, to say "Téo <u>plays</u> in the yard," we use で:

てお　は　にわ　で　あそびます。
TÉO　WA　NIWA　DE　ASOBIMASU

HELP NICO, TÉO AND EMILY FILL IN THE BLANKS IN THE FOLLOWING SENTENCES WITH EITHER *NI* に OR *DE* で TO INDICATE THE PLACE. YOU'LL FIND THE SOLUTIONS ON PAGE 125.

1. たぬきさん は いえ ＿＿＿ います。

2. てお は うみ ＿＿＿ いきます。

3. にこ は いえ ＿＿＿ にほんご を ならいます。

4. えみり と てお は にわ ＿＿＿ あそびます。

5. にこ は いえ ＿＿＿ かえります。

6. せんせい は みせ ＿＿＿ さいふ を かいます。

7. えみり は えき ＿＿＿ はがき を かきます。

8. たぬきさん は せんせい の いえ ＿＿＿ はいります。

9. にわ ＿＿＿ きますか。

10. にわ ＿＿＿ とり を みます。

11. たぬきさん は にほん ＿＿＿ すんでいます。

NEW WORDS...

さいふ
SAIFU
wallet

かえります
KAERIMASU
to come back home

すんで います
SUNDE IMASU
to live somewhere,
to inhabit

ME

MO

YU

These three *hiragana* ME め, MO も and YU ゆ should pose no particular problem.

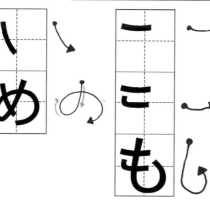

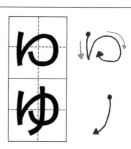

Yes, Emily, not only can you now wear a kimono, which you wear beautifully by the way (better than me!), but you can also write the word きもの.
If you want to know more about Japanese clothing, turn the page! Hmm, it fits you too, Nico. (Laughter)

CHAPTER 6: Traditional Japanese Clothes

The kimono is traditional Japanese formal wear. There are several varieties, each well adapted to the seasons and to the Japanese climate. You still see a lot of people dressed in kimono, especially older people, but in everyday life, the Japanese now wear clothes similar to our own. They only dress in kimono on special occasions: ceremonies, parties, etc. On these occasions, they also wear traditional footwear including the wooden flip-flops called *geta*, which you wear with special socks called *tabi*, which allow the big toe to be separated from the other toes. The

obi is the kimono's sash and some of these are
magnificently decorated and cost almost as much
as the kimono itself. Men wear a jacket called
haori over their kimono, as well as wide pants
called *hakama* during formal ceremonies.

In summer when it is warm, or inside hotels, the Japanese wear a very
light kimono called a *yukata*. During festivals, young people often wear a
hanten, a short jacket made of light fabric, and wear a bandana around
the forehead called a *hachimaki*.

る
RU

ろ
RO

The *hiragana* RU る and RO ろ also do not pose any problem: they are written with a single stroke and their shape is similar to our number 3. But be careful to differentiate between them: RU る ends with a little loop at the bottom.

くるま
KURUMA
car

さる
SARU
monkey

PRACTICE WRITING THE FOLLOWING WORDS:

ふろ
FURO
bath

しろ
SHIRO
castle

IN JAPANESE, TO SAY THAT YOU LIKE OR HATE SOMETHING, TWO SIMPLE EXPRESSIONS ARE USED:

(name of the person who likes)	は WA	(name of the person or thing liked)	が　すき　です。 GA　SUKI　DESU
(name of the person who hates)	は WA	(name of the person or thing hated)	が　きらい　です。 GA　KIRAI　DESU

YOU'LL NOTICE:
SOMETHING UNUSUAL HERE:
IN THESE EXPRESSIONS, THE DIRECT OBJECT IS NOT INDICATED BY THE PARTICLE を, BUT BY THE PARTICLE が!

BE CAREFUL ALSO OF THE PRONUNCIATION.
YOU HAVE TO PRONOUNCE KIRA-I CLEARLY WITH -I AT THE END AND SUKI IS REALLY PRONOUNCED SSSSKI WITHOUT THE U SOUND IN THE MIDDLE.

DO YOU UNDERSTAND WHAT EMILY, TÉO AND NICO ARE SAYING? YOU'LL FIND THE TRANSLATION ON PAGE 125.

わたし　は　すし　が　すき　です。たまご　が　きらい　です。

にこ　は　えみり　が　すき　です !!!!!!

てお　は　ばか　です。わたし　は　てお　が　きらい　です。

YA

YO

AND HERE ARE THE LAST TWO *HIRAGANA:* YA や AND YO よ! PAY ATTENTION TO THE ORDER OF THE STROKES SO THE CHARACTERS LOOK BALANCED!

よ!!

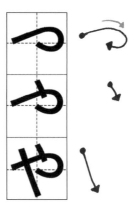

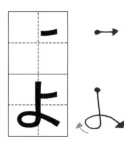

AND IT'S OVER! IT'S OVER!!!

NOT QUITE...!

WHAT?!!

88

YES, JUST A TINY DETAIL: IN THE SAME WAY THAT YOU CAN GET NEW SOUNDS BY ADDING TWO LITTLE DASHES ON THE TOP RIGHT OF SOME CHARACTERS, YOU CAN ALSO ADD A LITTLE CIRCLE ° TO THE TOP RIGHT OF THE CHARACTERS *HA* は, *HI* ひ, *FU* ふ, *HE* へ AND *HO* ほ TO GET THE NEW SOUNDS *PA* ぱ, *PI* ぴ, *PU* ぷ, *PE* ぺ AND *PO* ぽ! SIMPLE, ISN'T IT?

HA は	+ °	→	*PA* ぱ
HI ひ	+ °	→	*PI* ぴ
FU ふ	+ °	→	*PU* ぷ
HE へ	+ °	→	*PE* ぺ
HO ほ	+ °	→	*PO* ぽ

PHEW!!! I WAS WORRIED!!!

WHEW!! ME TOO! MASTER FOX, CAN I GO ぴ? I'M IN A BIG HURRY!!!

BEFORE WE GO ANY FURTHER, LET'S QUICKLY LEARN THREE SHORT WORDS THAT ARE VERY USEFUL. THE WORDS *KONO* この, *SONO* その AND *ANO* あの CORRESPOND TO OUR WORDS, *THIS, THESE, THAT* AND *THOSE*. PLACED BEFORE NOUNS, THEY ALLOW US TO REFER TO OBJECTS OR PEOPLE ACCORDING TO THEIR LOCATION.

KONO この, AS WELL AS *KORE* これ, INDICATES THINGS CLOSE TO THE SPEAKER; *SONO* その, AS WELL AS *SORE* それ, INDICATES THINGS CLOSE TO THE PERSON SPOKEN TO; AND *ANO* あの, AS WELL AS *ARE* あれ, INDICATES THINGS FAR FROM BOTH SPEAKERS. (SEE PAGE 62.)

あの　　やま　　は　　ふじさん　です。
ANO YAMA WA FUJISAN DESU
That mountain (over there) is Mount Fuji.

その　とり　は　すずめ　です。
SONO TORI WA SUZUME DESU
These birds are sparrows.

この　さかな　は　こい　です。
KONO SAKANA WA KOI DESU.
These fish are carp.

TANUKI-SAN HAS MIXED UP THE *HIRAGANA* AND HAS EVEN HIDDEN SEVERAL... ON PURPOSE! FIND THE MISSING ONES AND WITH THOSE, YOU'LL BE ABLE TO WRITE THE NAMES OF TWO JAPANESE CHILDREN WHO SHOULD BECOME EMILY, TÉO AND NICO'S FRIENDS IN NO TIME.

THE ORDER OF THE *HIRAGANA* IN THEIR NAMES IS THE ORDER IN WHICH THEY APPEAR IN THE CHART OF THE 46 SOUNDS (YOU'LL FIND THE SOLUTIONS ON PAGE 125.)

むおかよんくすぬそ
となにせねうのたし
をはるへまみわふめ
こりほもやあゆけさ
えらきてつれい

なまえ　は
NAMAE WA
＿＿＿です。
DESU

こりつれやゆのほも
えてたしさなにせね
みわふめうよちへま
はるひむいんくをろ
おかけすぬそと

なまえ　は
NAMAE WA
＿＿＿です。
DESU

91

SO... NOW I SUGGEST WE END OUR FIRST ENCOUNTER WITH THE JAPANESE LANGUAGE BY LEARNING A FEW *KANJI*. AS I TOLD YOU, JAPANESE IS WRITTEN BY COMBINING THE *HIRAGANA* ALPHABET AND *KANJI*. *KANJI* ARE THE CHINESE CHARACTERS THAT THE JAPANESE BORROWED FROM CHINA STARTING IN THE FIFTH CENTURY AND ADAPTED TO WRITE THEIR LANGUAGE. (LONG BEFORE THEY INVENTED *HIRAGANA* !)
UNLIKE *HIRAGANA* WHICH ARE PHONETIC LETTERS THAT EACH HAVE A SOUND (AND ONLY ONE) BUT NO MEANING ON THEIR OWN, *KANJI* ARE SYMBOLS THAT CAN HAVE ONE OR MORE MEANINGS, AS WELL AS ONE OR MORE PRONUNCIATIONS.

SHOOT! I HAD FORGOTTEN ABOUT THOSE!

BUT WHY DID THEY GO TO CHINA TO GET THESE CHARACTERS? DID THEY REALLY NEED THEM? WASN'T THERE A SIMPLER WAY? WERE THEY THAT BORED IN FIFTH-CENTURY JAPAN?! DON'T TELL ME THE ALPHABET DIDN'T EXIST!!!

CIVILIZATIONS THAT USED AN ALPHABET OF COURSE EXISTED, BUT WERE VERY FAR FROM JAPAN. AND CHINESE CIVILIZATION DOMINATED THAT PART OF THE WORLD, SO THE JAPANESE CHOSE WHAT SEEMED BEST FOR THEIR LANGUAGE.
HERE, WE'LL SIMPLY START BY LEARNING A FEW *KANJI* THAT ARE VERY SIMPLE AND WILL ALLOW US TO WRITE DOWN WORDS WE ALREADY KNOW. WE'LL SEE HOW THESE *KANJI* ARE USED TOGETHER WITH HIRAGANA.

SO WE'LL LEARN TO WRITE IN *KANJI* WHAT WE ALREADY KNOW HOW TO WRITE IN *HIRAGANA*, IS THAT IT?

YES, EMILY, IT'S A BIT LIKE THAT, BUT WHAT YOU'VE GOT TO UNDERSTAND (I KNOW IT'S HARD AT THE BEGINNING) IS THAT THE JAPANESE LANGUAGE <u>GAINS IN EFFICIENCY</u> WHEN IT'S WRITTEN COMBINING *HIRAGANA* AND *KANJI*, RATHER THAN WITH *HIRAGANA* ALONE.

HMMM...IF YOU SAY SO... OKAY, HOW DOES IT WORK?

In general, *kanji* come in four different varieties:

* Pictograms, which originally represented a drawing of something. For instance, the character for "mountain" is:

* Ideograms, which originally represented a simple idea. For instance, the character meaning "above" is:

一 → 丄 → 上 → 上

* Composites of simple characters, which combine the meanings of both. For instance, the pictograms for *moon* + *sun* combine to form a new character meaning "clarity":

* Phonetic characters, which combine one element giving the meaning and another giving information about its pronunciation. For instance, "time" is made up of the pictogram for *sun* or *day* 日, and the character 寺 that is added for its pronunciation *ji*. When you see the *kanji* 時 as part of a word, you can guess that it's probably pronounced *ji* (although there are exceptions).

TO GET AN IDEA HOW WRITTEN JAPANESE WORKS, LOOK AT HOW ENGLISH MIGHT BE WRITTEN USING A COMBINATION OF PICTOGRAMS, IDEOGRAMS AND PHONETIC SYMBOLS...

in the Mister

by the

At the ↑ of the , there are , and at the ↓

of the there are many . In the

100s of .

MASTER FOX WALKS IN THE YARD. TANUKI-SAN READS A BOOK BY THE POND. MASTER FOX SEES MOUNT FUJI. AT THE TOP OF THE MOUNTAIN, THERE ARE CLOUDS, AND AT THE BOTTOM, MANY TREES. IN THE SKY FLY HUNDREDS OF BIRDS.

94

---OR, MORE PRECISELY, IF WE WROTE ENGLISH BY MIXING *KANJI* SYMBOLS WITH THE LETTERS OF OUR ALPHABET (AS OPPOSED TO *HIRAGANA*) ACCORDING TO THE PRINCIPLES OF JAPANESE, IT WOULD LOOK SOMETHING LIKE THIS:

狐先生 歩 in the 庭 . Mister 狸 読 a 本

by the 池. 狐先生 見 富士山. At the 上 of the 山,

there are 雲, and at the 下 of the 山 there are many 森 .

In the 空 飛 百s of 鳥.

REMIND ME HERE...HOW MANY KANJI IN ALL? YOU TOLD US AT THE BEGINNING OF THE BOOK, BUT I CAN'T REMEMBER...

THE MOST COMPLETE DICTIONARIES INCLUDE AROUND 50,000...BUT...

---TWO THOUSAND ARE ENOUGH FOR MOST EVERYDAY USAGE. DURING SIX YEARS OF ELEMENTARY SCHOOL, JAPANESE CHILDREN LEARN EXACTLY 1,006 OF THEM; 170 PER YEAR ON AVERAGE.

I TOLD YOU HE DIDN'T REMEMBER!!!

NICE OF YOU, SENSEI, TO SCARE HIM LIKE THAT!

AS I MENTIONED EARLIER, KANJI CAN HAVE SEVERAL PRONUNCIATIONS (MOST HAVE TWO; SOME HAVE MORE). THE PRONUNCIATION DEPENDS ON THE MEANING YOU ARE USING. LET'S TAKE A SIMPLE EXAMPLE: THE KANJI FOR MOUNTAIN, 山. YOU WRITE IT WITH THREE STROKES, AND IT IS SOMETIMES READ YAMA AND SOMETIMES SAN.

山

YAMA/SAN

YES, LET'S GO FOR SIMPLE!

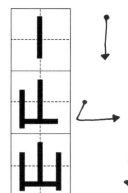

THIS KANJI IS READ YAMA やま WHEN IT IS USED BY ITSELF IN THE SENSE OF MOUNTAIN AND SAN WHEN IT IS COMBINED WITH THE NAME OF A PARTICULAR MOUNTAIN AS IS THE CASE OF FUJISAN ふじさん - "MOUNT FUJI."

ふじ山　は　にほん　の　山　です。
FUJISAN WA NIHON NO YAMA DESU
Mount Fuji is a Japanese ("of Japan") mountain.

HITO/JIN

LET'S TAKE ANOTHER EXAMPLE (EQUALLY SIMPLE, FOR TÉO'S SAKE): THE KANJI FOR "PERSON" 人 WHICH IS WRITTEN WITH TWO STROKES. IT IS SOMETIMES READ *HITO* AND SOMETIMES *JIN*.

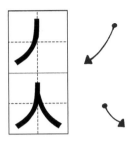

人 IS READ *HITO* ひと WHEN IT IS USED BY ITSELF TO MEAN PERSON. BUT WHEN 人 IS PART OF ANOTHER WORD IT IS OFTEN READ AS *JIN* じん. FOR EXAMPLE, IF YOU PUT THE KANJI 人 AT THE END OF THE NAME OF A COUNTRY IT IS READ *JIN* じん AND MEANS A PERSON WHO COMES FROM THAT COUNTRY. LOOK AT THESE TWO EXAMPLES:

この　　　人　　は　　にほん人　　　です。
KONO HITO WA NIHONJIN DESU
This person is Japanese.

あの　おんな　の　　人　　は　　あめりか人　です。
ANO ONNA NO HITO WA AMERIKAJIN DESU
That woman (over there) is American.

97

木
KI

川
KAWA

花
HANA

LET'S NOW LEARN SOME VERY SIMPLE *KANJI* THAT JAPANESE CHILDREN LEARN RIGHT OFF THE BAT. FOR EACH ONE, WE'LL LEARN ONLY ONE PRONUNCIATION FOR NOW, THE ONE USED TO WRITE WORDS WE ALREADY KNOW. THE FIRST, 木 (4 STROKES), IS READ *KI* AND MEANS "TREE"; THE SECOND, 川 (3 STROKES), IS READ *KAWA* AND MEANS "RIVER," AND THE THIRD, 花 (7 STROKES), IS READ *HANA* AND MEANS "FLOWER." PRACTICE WRITING THESE A FEW TIMES.

DON'T FORGET, JUST AS WITH THE *HIRAGANA*, YOU HAVE TO FOLLOW THE CORRECT STROKE ORDER!

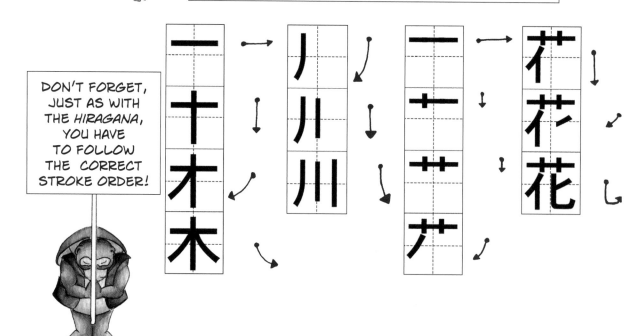

LET'S NOW SEE IF YOU'VE GOT IT. TRY FILLING IN THE BLANKS IN THE SENTENCES BELOW WITH THE *KANJI* YOU'VE JUST LEARNED. YOU'LL FIND THE CORRECT ANSWERS AND THE TRANSLATIONS OF THE SENTENCES ON PAGE 125.

やま
き
はな
□ に □ と □ が あります。

ひと
にわ に おんな の □ が います。

じん
えみり は あめりか □ です。

じん
さん
にほん □ は ふじ □ が すき です。

かわ
□ に さかな が います。

JUST AS WITH THE *HIRAGANA*, DON'T FORGET TO PRACTICE BY WRITING EACH *KANJI* LOTS OF TIMES ON GRID-MARKED PAPER!

男
OTOKO

女
ONNA

子
KO

THE FIRST OF THE THREE KANJI ABOVE, 男 (7 STROKES), IS READ *OTOKO* AND MEANS "MAN/MASCULINE"; THE SECOND, 女 (3 STROKES), IS READ *ONNA* AND MEANS "WOMAN/FEMININE"; AND THE THIRD, 子 (3 STROKES), IS READ *KO* AND MEANS "CHILD." THE FIRST TWO ARE VERY USEFUL FOR DISTINGUISHING THE BOYS' RESTROOM FROM THE GIRLS'!

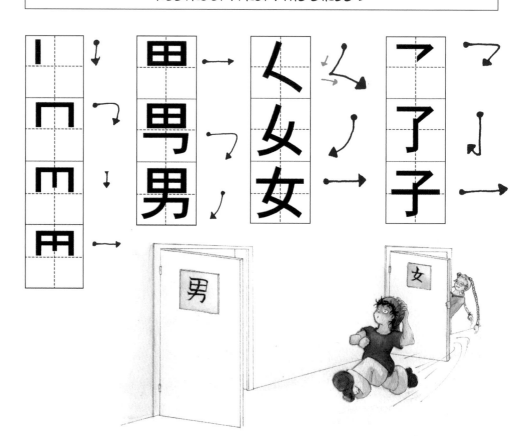

NEW WORDS...

むら
MURA
village

はなします
HANASHIMASU
to talk

わたし は ちひろ です。 にほん**人**
の **女** の **子** です。 にほんご を
はなします。 **山** の むら に すんで
います。 にほん の いなか です。
むら に いけ と **川** が あります。
わたし の にわ に **木** と **花** が
あります。 **木** は さくら です。
わたし の むら が すき です。

1. Who is the person behind the screen? _____

2. What language does this person speak? _____

3. Where does this person live? _____

4. What do we find where this person lives? _____

5. What kind of trees are there in this person's yard? _____

6. Does this person like or dislike where she/he lives? _____

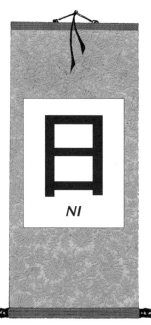

NI · HON

THE FIRST OF THESE TWO *KANJI*, 日 (4 STROKES), MEANS "SUN" AND IS READ *HI*. IT IS ALSO USED IN THE NAME *NIHON*, JAPAN, AND IN BOTH CASES IS READ *NI*. THE SECOND, 本 (5 STROKES), IS READ *HON* AND HAS TWO VERY DIFFERENT MEANINGS: IT MEANS EITHER "ORIGIN," OR... "BOOK." 本 IS WRITTEN JUST LIKE THE *KANJI* 木 (TREE), WITH AN EXTRA LITTLE HORIZONTAL DASH THAT'S DRAWN LAST.

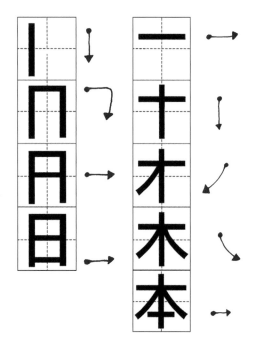

THE WORD *NIHON* 日本 MEANS "THE ORIGIN 本" OF THE "SUN 日." OF ALL THE ASIAN COUNTRIES, JAPAN IS THE MOST EASTWARD AND IS THE FIRST TO SEE THE SUN RISE IN THE MORNING. THAT'S WHY WE SOMETIMES CALL JAPAN THE "LAND OF THE RISING SUN."

102

この [ひと] は [に][ほん][じん] ではありません。

えみり は [き] と [はな] が すき です。

うみ で [おとこ] の [こ] と [おんな] の [こ] が あそびます。

この [に][ほん] の [やま] は ふじ [さん] です。

あめりか [じん] の [こ] は [に][ほん] の まんが が すき です。

犬
INU

猫
NEKO

魚
SAKANA

FINALLY, LET'S LEARN THREE *KANJI* USED IN NAMES OF VERY FAMILIAR ANIMALS. THE FIRST ONE, 犬 (4 STROKES), IS READ *INU* AND MEANS "DOG." THE SECOND, 猫 (11 STROKES!), IS READ *NEKO* AND MEANS "CAT." THE THIRD, 魚 (11 STROKES ALSO!) IS READ *SAKANA* AND MEANS "FISH."

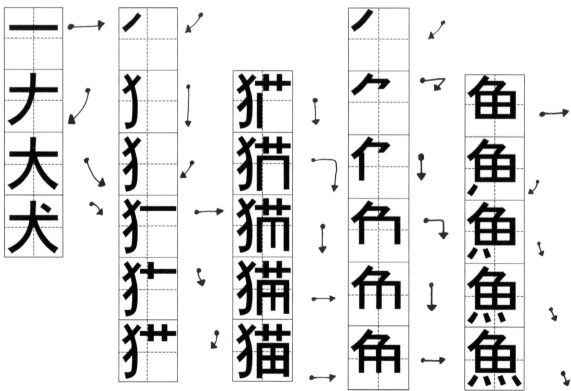

READ THE JAPANESE SENTENCES AT THE BOTTOM OF THE PAGE, THEN DRAW LINES TO CONNECT THE PEOPLE, THE ANIMALS AND THE OBJECTS ON THE FIRST TWO ROWS OF PICTURES BELOW TO THE PLACES ON THE BOTTOM TWO ROWS. SOME PEOPLE ANIMALS AND THINGS MAY BE IN MORE THAN ONE PLACE. YOU'LL FIND TRANSLATIONS OF THE SENTENCES ON PAGE 126.

犬 と 猫 は いえ に います。
さる は 木 で たべます。
男 の 人 は 山 に います。
魚 は 川 と いけ に います。
まんが は えき の みせ に あります。
日本人 の 女 の 人 は えき で 本 を かいます。
女 の 子 と 男 の 子 は にわ で あそびます。
とり は いけ に います。
花 は 山 と にわ に あります。

THE GOOD THING ABOUT WORDS WRITTEN IN *KANJI* IS THAT YOU CAN OFTEN GUESS THEIR MEANING. (IT'S MORE DIFFICULT TO GUESS THEIR EXACT PRONUNCIATION.) SO, WITHOUT WORRYING ABOUT HOW THE WORDS READ, TRY TO GUESS THE MEANINGS OF THE COMPOUND WORDS OF TWO KANJI BELOW, AND MATCH THEM TO THE ENGLISH WORDS. YOU'LL FIND THE CORRECT ANSWERS ON PAGE 126.

子犬	trees (plural)
人人	men and women
山川	kitten
山犬	river fish
木木	a pile of books
山山	wild cat
子猫	man in the mountains / mountain man
山人	persons/people (plural)
男女	wild dog
川魚	puppy dog
山猫	many mountains (plural)
本の山	mountain river

ON THE NEXT TWO PAGES, YOU'LL FIND THE JAPANESE *KANJI* NUMBERS FROM 1 TO 10. LEARN HOW TO WRITE THEM...AS YOU'LL SEE, THEY ARE NOT DIFFICULT. ALSO, LEARN THEIR PRONUNCIATIONS. (BUT BE CAREFUL: SOME CAN BE READ IN TWO DIFFERENT WAYS.)

ichi 1 一, *ni 2* 二, *san 3* 三, *shi or yon 4* 四, *go 5* 五, *roku 6* 六, *nana or shichi 7* 七, *hachi 8* 八, *kyuu 9* 九, *juu 10* 十.

Counting is very easy in Japanese:
11 is written 10 + 1, so it is 十一 *(juu ichi)*; likewise:
12 十二 *(juu ni)*; 13 十三 *(juu san)*; 14 十四 *(juu yon)*;
15 十五 *(juu go)*, etc.

20 is written 2 x 10 as in 二十 *(ni juu)*; so, 21 is 二十一 *(ni juu ichi)*; 22 二十二 *(ni juu ni)*; 23 二十三 *(ni juu san)*; 24 二十四 *(ni juu yon)*; 25 二十五 *(ni juu go)*, etc.

ON PAGES 120 AND 121 YOU'LL FIND A COMPLETE LIST OF THE NUMBERS FROM 1 TO 100. BEFORE CHECKING IT, TRY AND SEE IF YOU CAN FIGURE OUT THE FOLLOWING NUMBERS WRITTEN IN *KANJI*.

FOLLOWING THE DIRECTIONS KITSUNE-SENSEI GAVE YOU, CAN YOU FIGURE OUT HOW TO WRITE THESE NUMBERS IN JAPANESE? THE ANSWERS ARE ON PAGE 126.

四十三 → 43	二十三 →	68 → 六十八
二十八 →	九十九 →	24 →
五十六 →	八十七 →	19 →
十六 →	三十二 →	33 →
六十五 →	四十一 →	46 →
七十二 →	十七 →	97 →

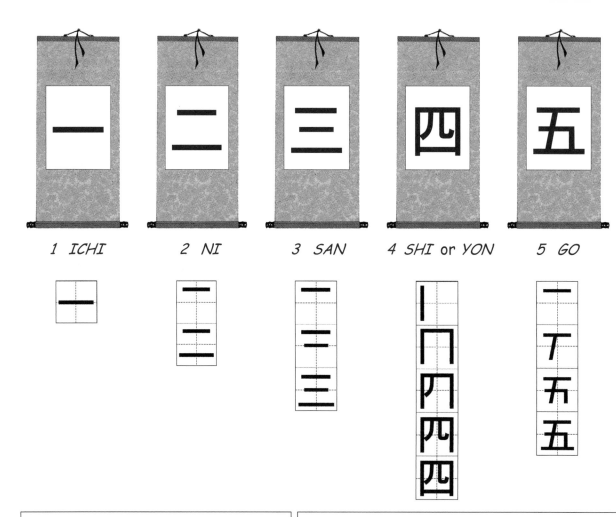

| 1 ICHI | 2 NI | 3 SAN | 4 SHI or YON | 5 GO |

To refer to someone's age, you add the suffix *sai* さい (pronounced sa-i) to the numbers we've just studied.

一さい one year old *I-SSSAI*
二さい two years old *NI-SAI*
三さい three years old *SAN-SAI*
四さい four years old *YON-SAI*
五さい five years old *GO-SAI*
六さい six years old *ROKU-SAI*
七さい seven years old *NANA-SAI*
八さい eight years old *HA-SSSAI*
九さい nine years old *KYUU-SAI*
十さい ten years old *JUU-SAI*

十一さい eleven years old *JUU-I-SSSAI*
十二さい twelve years old *JUU-NI-SAI*
十三さい thirteen years old *JUU-SAN-SAI*
十四さい fourteen years old *JUU-YON-SAI*
十五さい fifteen years old *JUU-GO-SAI*
...and so on..

HOW OLD ARE WE?
READ OUR AGES AND
CHECK YOUR ANSWERS
ON PAGE 127.

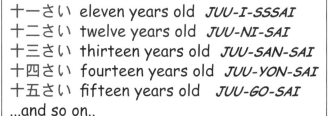

十一さい　です。

108

| 6 ROKU | 7 SHICHI or NANA | 8 HACHI | 9 KYUU | 10 JUU |

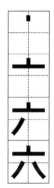

As you can see from the chart on the previous page, most ages are easy to say: 二さい *ni-sai*, 三さい *san-sai*, 四さい *yon-sai*, etc. Just don't forget to say sa-i as two separate sounds! There are however some special pronunciations: 一さい is pronounced *i-sssai* (you have to stress the sss) and not *ichi-sai*; the same goes for 十一さい which is pronounced *juu-i-sssai*; 八 さい is pronounced *ha-sssai* and not *hachi-sai*. Finally, take note that the word for "twenty years old" (the age when you become an adult in Japan) is *hatachi* without the *sai* and is written 二十.

十二さい　です。
たぬきさん　は
なん　さい　ですか。

二十五さい　です。

十二さい　です。

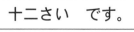

109

TO WRAP UP, LET'S LOOK AT SOME COMMON JAPANESE EXPRESSIONS. TRY TO READ THE FOLLOWING EXPRESSIONS AND GUESS WHAT THEY MEAN, WITH THE HELP OF THE ILLUSTRATIONS. THEN CHECK THEIR PRONUNCIATIONS AND MEANINGS IN THE BOX AT THE BOTTOM OF THE PAGE. (BEWARE: THERE ARE A FEW SPECIAL PRONUNCIATIONS... READ THEM CAREFULLY AND PRACTICE BY SAYING THEM OUT LOUD.)

どうも　ありがとう　ございます。

どういたしまして。

どうも　ありがとう…

ありがとう。

どうも…

From top to bottom. *Doumo arigatou gozaimasu* (pronounce the i of *gozaimasu* well and don't pronounce the final *u* sound but rather say *masss*): "Thank you very much!" One can also say, more colloquially, *doumo arigatou* or *arigatou* or even *doumo*: "Thank you." Dou *itashimashite* is equivalent to our "Welcome" or "You're welcome."

110

おはよう
ございます。

おはよう…

こんにちは…

こんにちは…
せんせい…

こんばんは…

こんばんは…

おやすみ なさい…

おやすみ…

From top to bottom. *Ohayou gozaimasu*
(pronounce carefully the *i* of *gozaimasu*, without
emphasis on the final *u* sound: *masss...*): "Good
morning!" *Konnichiwa* (は is read *wa* here): "Good
day!" *Konbanwa* (は is read *wa* here also): "Good
evening!" *Oyasumi nasai* (pay attention to the final
i sound): "Good night!"

From top to bottom: *Sumimasen* is used to grab someone's attention: "Excuse me!" or "Please!" in order to ask for information or to order something in a restaurant. *Sumimasen* is also used to excuse oneself: "Excuse me… (for having done something wrong)." *Gomen nasai* (pronounce the i properly) also means "Excuse me," "Forgive me." *Genki desu ka* asks about health: "Are you fine?", "How are you?" Emily is saying that she's fine, and Téo that he's not well…

From top to bottom: *Itadakimasu* (do not pronounce the final *u* sound: *masss...*) means literally "Thank you for this meal (of which I am about to partake)" and everyone says it aloud before starting to eat. *Takusan meshiagare* means literally "Eat a lot" and corresponds to "Bon appétit," but is usually said by the person who is offering or has prepared the meal. *Dewa mata* (here also は is pronounced *wa*) is equivalent to "See you"; and *sayounara* means "Goodbye."

いただきます!!!!!!

たくさん　めしあがれ!!!

では　また…

さようなら…

EMILY, TÉO AND NICO HAVE RECEIVED A LETTER FROM JAPAN. CAN YOU HELP THEM READ AND UNDERSTAND IT? YOU'LL FIND THE MEANINGS OF WORDS YOU DON'T REMEMBER AND OF SOME NEW WORDS (MARKED BY A *) IN THE VOCABULARY PAGES AT THE END OF THE BOOK.

こんにちは。

なまえ は あきら です。あめりか人 で は ありません。日本人 の 男 の 子 です。 十二さい です。 ちひろ の あに* です。 ちひろ は 十さい の 女 の 子 です。

日本 の 山 の むら に すんでいます。 いえ は いなか に あります。 にわ が あります。 木 と 花 が たくさん* あります。にわ で わたし と ちひろ は あそびます。 この にわ が すき です。

はは* は かんごふ* です。 ちち* は えいご の せんせい です。 しかし*、 わたし は えいご を はなしません。

わたし の いえ に 犬 と 猫 が います。 犬 の なまえ は くろ* です。 猫 の なまえ は ゆき* です。

わたし は まんが と 本 が すき です。 山 と おんせん が すき です。 しかし*、 うみ と まち* が きらい です。

みなさん* は だれ ですか。 どこ に すんでいますか。どこ の くに* ですか。 なんさい ですか。 男 の 子 ですか。女 の 子 ですか。にほんご を はなしますか。

なに が すき ですか。 なに が きらい ですか。

みなさん* は わたし の ともだち* に, なりますか*。

さようなら。

あきら

わたし の かぞく*

ちち

はは

くろ

わたし ゆき ちひろ

AFTER READING THIS LETTER, CAN YOU ANSWER THE FOLLOWING QUESTIONS? YOU'LL FIND THE ANSWERS AND THE TRANSLATION OF THE ENTIRE LETTER ON PAGE 127.

1. Who wrote the letter? _____

2. What is the citizenship of this person? _____

3. How old is the author of the letter? _____

4. What other person is talked about at the beginning of the letter? _____

5. Does the author know the other person well? _____

   Why? _____

6. How old is the other person? _____

7. Where does the author live? _____

8. Does the author have a yard? If so, what is in it? _____

9. What does the author do in the yard? With whom? _____

10. Who are the other two people mentioned in the letter? _____

11. What is their occupation? _____

12. What language(s) does the author speak? _____

13. Does he/she have animals in the home? Which ones? _____

14. What are their names? _____

15. Why do you think they were given those names? _____

16. What does the author like? _____

17. What does she/he hate? _____

18. Who is he/she speaking to at the end of the letter? _____

19. What does he/she want to know? _____

20. What does she/he suggest? _____

TRY TO WRITE THE REPLIES THAT EMILY, TÉO AND NICO SEND TO AKIRA IN JAPANESE. ALSO INTRODUCE YOURSELF BY ANSWERING THE QUESTIONS ASKED BY AKIRA AT THE END OF THE LETTER.

?

SO, WE'RE DONE FOR NOW. WE'VE LEARNED LOTS OF THINGS TOGETHER. BUT YOUR STUDY OF THE JAPANESE LANGUAGE IS OF COURSE FAR FROM OVER... STUDY WHAT YOU'VE LEARNED IN THIS BOOK, PRACTICE WRITING THE *HIRAGANA* AND THE *KANJI* I'VE SHOWN YOU... AND IF YOU'VE ENJOYED THIS AND FOUND IT INTERESTING, JOIN US AGAIN SOON...

では　また　…

IN ORDER TO HELP YOU, TANUKI-SAN HAS COMPILED A LIST OF ALL THE VOCABULARY WE'VE STUDIED IN THIS BOOK. THEY ARE LISTED IN THE ORDER OF THE 46 JAPANESE SOUNDS (AS IN THE CHART YOU'VE STUDIED): *A* あ, *I* い, *U* う, *E* え, *O* お, *KA* か, *KI* き, *KU* く, *KE* け, *KO* こ, *SA* さ, *SHI* し, *SU* す, *SE* せ, *SO* そ AND SO ON.

VOCABULARY LIST

あ a

あきら : *AKIRA* (boy's name)

あそびます : *ASOBIMASU* to play

あなた : *ANATA* you

あなたたち : *ANATATACHI* you (plural)

あに : *ANI* older brother

あの : *ANO* that, those over there (far from both speakers), describing word

あめりか : *AMERIKA* America

あめりかじん/あめりか人 : *AMERIKAJIN* an American person

あり : *ARI* ant

ありがとう : *ARIGATOU* thank you

あります : *ARIMASU* to be, to exist (for inanimate objects: things, items)

あれ : *ARE* that thing, those things over there (far from both speakers)

い i

いいえ : *IIE* "no"

いえ : *IE* house

いきます : *IKIMASU* to go

いし : *ISHI* stone

いす : *ISU* chair

いただきす : *IKIMASU* "thank you for this meal (which I am about to eat)" (You say this before you begin to eat.)

いとこ : *ITOKO* cousin

いなか : *INAKA* countryside

いぬ : *INU* dog

いね : *INE* rice grass

います : *IMASU* to be, to exist (for living things: animals, humans)

いわ : *IWA* rock

117

う u

うみ：*UMI* sea
うた：*UTA* song

え e

えいご：*EIGO* the English language
えき：*EKI* train station
えだ：*EDA* tree branch

お o

おかし：*OKASHI* candy, sweets
おとこ/男：*OTOKO* man/masculine
おとこ の こ/男の子：*OTOKO NO KO* boy
おとこのひと/男の人：*OTOKO NO HITO*
man, male person
おはよう ございます：*OHAYOU
GOZAIMASU* "good morning"
おび：*OBI* kimono sash
おやすみ なさい：*OYASUMI NASAI* "good
night"
おんせん：*ONSEN* hot spring bath
おんな/女：*ONNA* woman/feminine
おんな のこ/女の子：*ONNA NO KO* girl,
little girl
おんな のひと/女の人：*ONNA NO HITO*
woman, female person

か ka

か：*KA* (question particle that comes at the
end of a sentence)
が：*GA* (particle indicating a verb's subject)
かいます：*KAIMASU* to buy
かえります：*KAERIMASU* to return home
(to your house or to your country)
かぎ：*KAGI* key
かきます：*KAKIMASU* to write
かぞく：*KAZOKU* family
かね：*KANE* bell
かばん：*KABAN* bag, schoolbag
かみ：*KAMI* 1. god, Japanese divinity;
2. (different kanji) paper, sheet of paper
からだ：*KARADA* body
からて：*KARATE* karate
かわ/川：*KAWA* river
かんごふ：*KANGOFU* nurse
かんじ：*KANJI* (Chinese characters)

き ki

き/木：*KI* tree
ききます：*KIKIMASU* to listen
きつね：*KITSUNE* fox
きます：*KIMASU* to come
きもの：*KIMONO* kimono
きらい です：*KIRAI DESU* to hate

く ku

くに：*KUNI* country
くるま：*KURUMA* car
くろ：*KURU* black

け ke

げた：*GETA* (traditional wooden flip-flops)
げんき です：*GENKI DESU* "I'm fine..."
げんき ですか：*GENKI DESU KA* "How are
you?"

こ ko

こ/子：*KO* child
こい：*KOI* carp
この：*KONO* this, these (close to the
speaker), describing word
ごめん なさい：*GOMEN NASAI* "sorry,"
"excuse me"
これ：*KORE* this thing, these things here
(close to the speaker)
こんにちは：*KONNICHIWA* "good day" (は
is pronounced *WA*)
こんばんは：*KONBANWA* "good evening" (は
is pronounced *WA*)

さ sa

さかな/魚：*SAKANA* fish
さくら：*SAKURA* cherry tree
さしみ：*SASHIMI* (slices of raw fish)
ざぜん：*ZAZEN* (meditation pose in Zen)
さようなら：*SAYOUNARA* "goodbye"
さる：*SARU* monkey
-さん：*-SAN* Mr., Mrs., Miss

し shi

しかし：*SHIKASHI* but
します：*SURU* to do
しろ：*SHIRO* castle

す su

すき です : *SUKI DESU* to like

すし : *SUSHI* sushi

すずめ : *SUZUME* sparrow

すみません : *SUMIMASEN* 1. "excuse me!", "please!" (to attract someone's attention) 2. "excuse me" for having done something wrong

すもう : *SUMO* sumo (In Japanese, stretch out the final o sound)

すんでいます : *SUNDE IMASU* to inhabit, to live in

せ se

ぜん : *ZEN* Zen (religion: one form of Buddhism)

せんせい : *SENSEI* master, professor, teacher

そ so

その : *SONO* that, those (close to the person spoken to), describing word

それ : *SORE* that thing, those things (close to the person spoken to)

た ta

たき : *TAKI* waterfall

たくさん : *TAKUSAN* a lot

たくさん　めしあがれ : *TAKUSAN MESHIAGARE* "eat a lot" ("bon appétit!")

たたみ : *TATAMI* (rice-straw mats that cover the floor in Japanese houses)

たぬき : *TANUKI* (raccoon-dog native to Japan and Asia)

たび : *TABI* (traditional Japanese sock in which the big toe is split from the other toes)

たべます : *TABEMASU* to eat

たまご : *TAMAGO* egg

だれ : *DARE* who?

ち chi

ちち : *CHICHI* (my) father

ちひろ : *CHIHIRO* (girl's name)

つ tsu

つかれました : *TSUKAREMASHITA* to be tired

つき : *TSUKI* moon

つなみ : *TSUNAMI* tsunami

て te

て : *TE* hand

で : *DE* at or in

てがみ : *TEGAMI* letter (mail)

です : *DESU* is or are

では また : *DEWA MATA* "See you soon"

てら : *TERA* temple, Buddhist monastery

でんき : *DENKI* electricity

でんわ : *DENWA* telephone

と to

どう いたしまして : *DOU ITASHIMASHITE* "welcome," "with pleasure"

どうも : *DOUMO* "thank you"

どうも ありがとう : *DOUMO ARIGATOU* "thank you very much"

どこ : *DOKO* where?

ともだち : *TOMODACHI* friend

ともだち に なります : *TOMODACHI NI NARIMASU* to become friends

とり : *TORI* bird

な na

なに : *NANI* what?

なまえ : *NAMAE* name

ならいます : *NARAIMASU* to learn

なります : *NARIMASU* to become

なん : *NANI* what

に ni

に : *NI* to or in (a place)

にほん/日本 : *NIHON* Japan

にほんご : *NIHONGO* Japanese language

にほんじん/日本人 : *NIHONJIN* a Japanese person

にわ : *NIWA* yard

ね ne

ねこ/猫 : *NEKO* cat

の no

の : *NO* of

は ha/wa

は : *WA* particle indicating the topic of the sentence)
はい : *HAI* yes
はいります : *HAIRIMASU* to enter
はおり : *HAORI* (traditional jacket worn over kimono)
ばか : *BAKA* stupid
はかま : *HAKAMA* (traditional wide pants)
はがき : *HAGAKI* postcard
はこ : *HAKO* box
はし : *HASHI* 1. chopsticks, 2. (different kanji) bridge
はた : *HATA* flag
はちまき : *HACHIMAKI* bandanna
はな/花 : *HANA* flower
はなします : *HANASHIMASU* to talk
はは : *HAHA* (my) mother
はま : *HAMA* beach
はんてん : *HANTEN* (traditional short jacket)

ひ hi

ひと/人 : *HITO* (a) person
ひらがな : *HIRAGANA* hiragana

ふ fu

ふじさん/ふじ山 : *FUJISAN* Mount Fuji
ふろ : *FURO* bath

ほ ho

ほん/本 : *HON* book

ま ma

まきこ : *MAKIKO* (girl's name)
まち : *MACHI* town
まんが : *MANGA* manga

み mi

みせ : *MISE* shop
みなさん : *MINASAN* all, everyone
みます : *MIMASU* to see

む mu

むら : *MURA* village

や mo

やま/山 : *YAMA* mountain

ゆ yu

ゆかた : *YUKATA* (light summer kimono)
ゆき : *YUKI* snow

よ yo

よこずな : *YOKOZUNA* (sumo champion)

り ri

りきし : *RIKISHI* sumo wrestler

わ wa

わたし : *WATASHI* I, me

を o

を : (particle that indicates the direct object)

JAPANESE NUMBERS FROM 1 TO 100

1	一	*ICHI*	11	十一	*JUU ICHI*
2	二	*NI*	12	十二	*JUU NI*
3	三	*SAN*	13	十三	*JUU SAN*
4	四	*YON* or *SHI*	14	十四	*JUU YON*
5	五	*GO*	15	十五	*JUU GO*
6	六	*ROKU*	16	十六	*JUU ROKU*
7	七	*NANA* or *SHICHI*	17	十七	*JUU NANA*
8	八	*HACHI*	18	十八	*JUU HACHI*
9	九	*KYUU*	19	十九	*JUU KYUU*
10	十	*JUU*	20	二十	*NI JUU*

21	二十一	*NI JUU ICHI*	61	六十一	*ROKU JUU ICHI*
22	二十二	*NI JUU NI*	62	六十二	*ROKU JUU NI*
23	二十三	*NI JUU SAN*	63	六十三	*ROKU JUU SAN*
24	二十四	*NI JUU YON*	64	六十四	*ROKU JUU YON*
25	二十五	*NI JUU GO*	65	六十五	*ROKU JUU GO*
26	二十六	*NI JUU ROKU*	66	六十六	*ROKU JUU ROKU*
27	二十七	*NI JUU NANA*	67	六十七	*ROKU JUU NANA*
28	二十八	*NI JUU HACHI*	68	六十八	*ROKU JUU HACHI*
29	二十九	*NI JUU KYUU*	69	六十九	*ROKU JUU KYUU*
30	三十	*SAN JUU*	70	七十	*NANA JUU*
31	三十一	*SAN JUU ICHI*	71	七十一	*NANA JUU ICHI*
32	三十二	*SAN JUU NI*	72	七十二	*NANA JUU NI*
33	三十三	*SAN JUU SAN*	73	七十三	*NANA JUU SAN*
34	三十四	*SAN JUU YON*	74	七十四	*NANA JUU YON*
35	三十五	*SAN JUU GO*	75	七十五	*NANA JUU GO*
36	三十六	*SAN JUU ROKU*	76	七十六	*NANA JUU ROKU*
37	三十七	*SAN JUU NANA*	77	七十七	*NANA JUU NANA*
38	三十八	*SAN JUU HACHI*	78	七十八	*NANA JUU HACHI*
39	三十九	*SAN JUU KYUU*	79	七十九	*NANA JUU KYUU*
40	四十	*YON JUU*	80	八十	*HACHI JUU*
41	四十一	*YON JUU ICHI*	81	八十一	*HACHI JUU ICHI*
42	四十二	*YON JUU NI*	82	八十二	*HACHI JUU NI*
43	四十三	*YON JUU SAN*	83	八十三	*HACHI JUU SAN*
44	四十四	*YON JUU YON*	84	八十四	*HACHI JUU YON*
45	四十五	*YON JUU GO*	85	八十五	*HACHI JUU GO*
46	四十六	*YON JUU ROKU*	86	八十六	*HACHI JUU ROKU*
47	四十七	*YON JUU NANA*	87	八十七	*HACHI JUU NANA*
48	四十八	*YON JUU HACHI*	88	八十八	*HACHI JUU HACHI*
49	四十九	*YON JUU KYUU*	89	八十九	*HACHI JUU KYUU*
50	五十	*GO JUU*	90	九十	*KYUU JUU*
51	五十一	*GO JUU ICHI*	91	九十一	*KYUU JUU ICHI*
52	五十二	*GO JUU NI*	92	九十二	*KYUU JUU NI*
53	五十三	*GO JUU SAN*	93	九十三	*KYUU JUU SAN*
54	五十四	*GO JUU YON*	94	九十四	*KYUU JUU YON*
55	五十五	*GO JUU GO*	95	九十五	*KYUU JUU GO*
56	五十六	*GO JUU ROKU*	96	九十六	*KYUU JUU ROKU*
57	五十七	*GO JUU NANA*	97	九十七	*KYUU JUU NANA*
58	五十八	*GO JUU HACHI*	98	九十八	*KYUU JUU HACHI*
59	五十九	*GO JUU KYUU*	99	九十九	*KYUU JUU KYUU*
60	六十	*ROKU JUU*	100	百	*HYAKU*

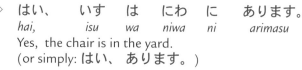

page 28

Japanese は ^(wa) raw fish を ^(o) to like か ^(ka).
Yes, Japanese は ^(wa) raw fish を ^(o) to like.
Tanuki-san は ^(wa) where に ⁽ⁿⁱ⁾ to go か ^(ka).
Tanuki-san は ^(wa) yard に ⁽ⁿⁱ⁾ to go.

page 36

はな *hana* (flower); き *ki* (tree); さかな *sakana* (fish); いね *ine* (young rice shoot);
いし *ishi* (stone); いわ *iwa* (rock); はた *hata* (flag); いぬ *inu* (dog); つき *tsuki* (moon);
かね *kane* (bell); いなか *inaka* (countryside); たき *taki* (waterfall); はし *hashi* (bridge)

page 46

ねこ	は	にわ	に	います。
1. neko	wa	niwa	ni	imasu
cat		yard		to be

The cat is in the yard.

いぬ	は	いえ	に	います。
2. inu	wa	ie	ni	imasu
dog		house		to be

The dog is in the house.

あり	は	き	に	います。
3. ari	wa	ki	ni	imasu
ant		tree		to be

The ants are in the tree.

さかな	は	かわ	に	います。
4. sakana	wa	kawa	ni	imasu
fish		river		to be

The fish are in the river.

はた	は	はま	に	あります。
5. hata	wa	hama	ni	arimasu
flag		beach		to be

The flag is on the beach.

かね	は	てら	に	あります。
6. kane	wa	tera	ni	arimasu
bell		temple		to be

The bell is in the temple.

page 47

1. *Kitsune-sensei wa ie ni* **imasu**.
   Kitsune-sensei is in the house.

2. *Taki wa ni* **arimasu**.
   The waterfall is in the yard.

3. *Tanuki-san wa hama ni* **imasu**.
   Tanuki-san is on the beach.

4. *Teo wa ki ni* **imasu**.
   Téo is in the tree.

5. *Iwa wa kawa ni* **arimasu**.
   The rocks are in the river.

6. *Ki wa niwa ni* **arimasu**.
   The trees are in the yard.

page 52

はた	は	にわ	に	ありますか。
hata	wa	niwa	ni	arimasuka

Is the flag in the yard?

⇨

いいえ、	はた	は	にわ	に	ありません。
iie,	hata	wa	niwa	ni	arimasen

No, the flag is not in the yard.
(or simply: いいえ、ありません。)

いす	は	にわ	に	ありますか。
isu	wa	niwa	ni	arimasuka

Is the chair in the yard?

⇨

はい、	いす	は	にわ	に	あります。
hai,	isu	wa	niwa	ni	arimasu

Yes, the chair is in the yard.
(or simply: はい、あります。)

はな	は	にわ	に	ありますか。
hana	wa	niwa	ni	arimasuka

Are the flowers in the yard?

⇨

いいえ、	はな	は	にわ	に	ありません。
iie,	hana	wa	niwa	ni	arimasen

No, the flowers are not in the yard.
(or simply: いいえ、ありません。)

					⇨						

てお　　は　　いえ　　に　　いますか。　⇨　いいえ、てお　　は　　いえ　　に　　いません。
Téo　wa　ie　ni　imasuka　　　　iie,　Téo　wa　ie　ni　imasen
Is Téo in the house?　　　　　　　No, Téo is not in the house.
　　　　　　　　　　　　　　　　　　(or simply: いいえ、いません。)

いぬ　　は　　かわ　　に　　いますか。　⇨　いいえ、いぬ　　は　　かわ　　に　　いません。
inu　wa　kawa　ni　imasuka　　　　iie,　inu　wa　kawa　ni　imasen
Is the dog in the river?　　　　　　No, the dog is not in the river.
　　　　　　　　　　　　　　　　　　(or simply: いいえ、いません。)

にこ　　は　　き　　に　　いますか。　⇨　はい、にこ　　は　　き　　に　　います。
Nico　wa　ki　ni　imasuka　　　　hai,　Nico　wa　ki　ni　imasu
Is Nico in the tree?　　　　　　　Yes, Nico is in the tree.
　　　　　　　　　　　　　　　　　　(or simply: はい、います。)

page 53

1 *hashi* = D and H; 2 *eki* = E; 3 *inu* = F; 4 *mise* = B; 5 *hama* = G; 6 *tsuki* = C; 7 *inaka* = A.

A: tsunami　　　　B: karate

page 57 (going in columns, from top to bottom and from left to right):

tamago (egg)	*manga* (manga)	*hagaki* (postcard)	*denwa* (telephone)
karada (body)	*tegami* (letter, mail)	*kagi* (keys)	*kanji* (kanji)
kaban (bag)	*denki* (electricity)	*eda* (branch)	*zazen* (meditation pose)

page 59

Emily: *Namae wa Emily desu. Ie ni imasen. Onsen ni imasu.* My name is Emily. I am not in the house. I am in the hot spring.

Téo: *Watashi wa Nico dewa arimasen. Téo desu. Niwa ni imasu.* I am not Nico. My name is Téo. I am in the yard.

Nico: *Watashi wa ie ni imasu. Namae wa Nico desu. Ie wa inaka ni arimasu.* I am in the house. My name is Nico. The house is in the countryside.

page 63

A. です 6	C. です 8	E. います 7	G. あります 4	I. います 3
B. います 10	D. です 9	F. あります 2	H. です 1	J. あります 5

page 65

1-B (*Nico!! Kore wa nan desu ka.* Nico!!! What is this?)
2-E (*Kore wa hon desu, Sensei.* It's a book, Sensei.)
3-F (*Iie, manga desu!!* No, it's a manga!!!)

4-C (*Nico wa baka desu.* Nico is stupid.)
5-A (*Kami wa doko ni arimasuka.* Where are the papers?)
6-D (*Isu ni imasu.* They're on the chair.)

page 66

Emily: *Sensei to Tanuki-san wa niwa ni arimasuka.* Are Sensei and Tanuki-san in the yard?
Téo: *Iie, imasen. Ie ni imasu.* No, they're not. They're in the house.
Emily: *Kore wa nan desu ka.* What is this?
Téo: *Sore wa hon to manga desu.* These are books and manga.
Téo: *Sore wa nan desu ka.* What's that?
Emily: *Tegami to hagaki desu.* Those are letters and postcards.

page 70

To eat:	たべます	にこ	は	すし	を	たべます。
		Nico	*wa*	*sushi*	*o*	*tabemasu*

Nico is eating sushi.

To do:	します	えみり	は	なに	を	しますか。
		Emily	*wa*	*nani*	*o*	*shimasuka*

What is Emily doing?

To buy:	かいます	てお	は	まんが	を	かいます。
		Téo	*wa*	*manga*	*o*	*kaimasu*

Téo buys manga.

To learn:	ならいます	わたし	は	にほんご	を	ならいます。
		watashi	*wa*	*nihongo*	*o*	*naraimasu*

I'm learning Japanese.

To look at:	みます	きつねせんせい	は	ふじさん	を	みます。
		Kitsune-sensei	*wa*	*Fujisan*	*o*	*mimasu*

Master Fox looks at Mount Fuji.

To write:	かきます	にこ	は	てがみ	を	かきます。
		Nico	*wa*	*tegami*	*o*	*kakimasu*

Nico writes a letter.

To listen:	ききます	えみり	は	うた	を	ききます。
		Emily	*wa*	*uta*	*o*	*kikimasu*

Emily listens to a song.

page 74

これ は わたし の かばん です。
Kore wa watashi no kaban desu. This is my schoolbag.

きつねせんせい と たぬきさん は にわ に います。
Kitsune-sensei to Tanuki-san wa niwa ni imasu. Kitsune-sensei and Tanunki-san are in the yard.

にこ と てお は あめりかじん です。
Nico to Téo wa Amerikajin desu. Nico and Téo are American.

てお は ほん と まんが を かいます。
Téo wa hon to manga o kaimasu. Téo buys books and manga.

わたし の いえ は いなか に あります。
Watashi no ie wa inaka ni arimasu. My house is in the countryside.

えみり の はし は これ です。
Emily no hashi wa kore desu. These are Emily's chopsticks.

にこ は うた を ききます。
Nico wa uta o kikimasu. Nico listens to a song.

1. が. What's on the chair?
   *Isu ni nani **ga** arimasuka.*
2. が. There are manga.
   *Manga **ga** arimasu.*
3. は. Whose manga are they?
   *Manga **wa** dare no manga desu ka.*
4.   These are my manga.
   Watashi no manga desu.
5. は. What is this? Is this a manga?
   *Kore **wa** nan desu ka. Manga desu ka.*
6. は. No, this is a Japanese book.
   *Iie, kore **wa** Nihongo no hon desu.*
7. が. Is there a cherry tree in the yard?
   *Niwa ni sakura **ga** arimasuka.*
8.   Yes, there is.
   Hai, arimasu.

1. に; *Tanuki-san wa ie **ni** imasu.* Tanunki-san is at home.
2. に; *Téo wa umi **ni** ikimasu.* Téo goes to the beach.
3. で; *Nico wa ie **de** Nihongo o naraimasu.* Nico studies Japanese at home.
4. で; *Emily to Téo wa niwa **de** asobimasu.* Emily and Téo play in the yard.
5. に; *Nico wa ie **ni** kaerimasu.* Nico goes back home.
6. で; *Sensei wa mise **de** saifu o kaimasu.* The teacher buys a wallet in a store.
7. で; *Emily wa eki **de** hagaki o kakimasu.* Emily writes postcards at the train station.
8. に; *Tanuki-san ha sensei no ie **ni** hairimasu.* Tanunki-san goes into the teacher's house.
9. に; *Niwa **ni** kimasuka.* Will you come in the yard?
10. で; *Niwa **de** tori o mimasu.* I watch birds in the yard.
11. に; *Tanuki-san Nihon **ni** sunde imasu.* Tanuki-san lives in Japan.

Nico: *Watashi wa sushi ga suki desu. Tamago ga kirai desu.* I like sushi. I don't like eggs.
Téo: *Nico wa Emily ga suki desu!!!!!* Nico likes Emily!!!!!
Emily: *Téo wa baka desu. Téo ga kirai desu.* Téo is stupid. I don't like Téo.

Girl: ちひろ (Chihiro)   Boy: あきら (Akira)

山 に 木 と 花 が あります。
(*Yama ni ki to hana ga arimasu.* There are trees and flowers on the mountain.)

にわ に おんな の 人 が います。
(*Niwa ni onna no hito ga imasu.* There's a woman in the yard.)

えみり は あめりか人 です。
(*Emily wa Amerikajin desu.* Emily is American.)

にほん人 は ふじ山 が すき です。
(*Nihonjin wa Fujisan ga suki desu.* The Japanese love Mount Fuji.)

川 に さかな が います 。
(*Kawa ni sakana ga imasu.* There are fish in the river.)

Watashi wa Chihiro desu. Nihonjin no onna no ko desu. Nihongo o hanashimasu. Yama no mura ni sunde imasu. Nihon no inaka desu. Mura ni ike to kawa ga arimasu. Watashi no niwa ni ki to hana ga arimasu. Ki wa sakura desu. Watashi no mura ga suki desu.

I'm Chihiro. I'm a Japanese girl. I speak Japanese. I live in a mountain village. It's in the Japanese countryside. In the village there's a pond and a river. In my garden there are trees and flowers. The trees are cherry trees. I like my village.

1. It's a girl whose name is Chihiro.
2. She speaks Japanese.
3. She lives in a mountainous village of Japan.
4. There we find a pond and a river.
5. Cherry trees.
6. She likes her village.

page 103

この 人 は 日本人 では ありません。
(*Kono hito wa Nihonjin dewa arimasen.* This person is not Japanese.)
えみり は 木 と 花 が すき です。
(*Emily wa ki to hana ga suki desu.* Emily likes trees and flowers.)
うみ で 男 の 子 と 女 の 子 が あそびます。
(*Umi de otoko no ko to onna no ko ga asobimasu.* Boys and girls are playing by the sea.)
この 日本 の 山 は ふじ山 です。
(*Kono Nihon no yama wa Fujisan desu.* This Japanese mountain is Mount Fuji.)
あめりか人 の 子 は 日本 の まんが が すき です。
(*Amerikajin no ko wa Nihon no manga ga suki desu.* American children like Japanese manga.)

page 105

Inu to neko wa ie ni imasu. The dog and the cat are in the house.
Saru wa ki de tabemasu. The monkey eats in the tree.
Otoko no hito wa yama ni imasu. There's a man in the mountain.
Sakana wa kawa to ike ni imasu. There are fish in the river and the pond.
Manga wa eki no mise ni arimasu. There are manga in the train station shop.
Nihonjin no onna no hito wa eki de hon o kaimasu. The Japanese woman buys books at the station.
Onna no ko to otoko no ko wa niwa de asobimasu. A girl and a boy are playing in the yard.
Tori wa ike ni imasu. There's a bird by the pond.
Hana wa yama to niwa ni arimasu. There are flowers in the mountain and in the yard.

page 106

子犬	puppy dog
人人	people/persons (plural): (1 person + 1 person = several *persons)
山川	mountain river
山犬	wild dog (literally: mountain dog)
木木	trees (plural): (1 tree + 1 tree = trees*)
山山	mountains (plural): (1 mountain + 1 mountain = mountains*)
子猫	kitten
山人	man living in the mountain/mountain man
男女	men and women
川魚	river fish
山猫	wild cat (literally: mountain cat)
本の山	a pile of books (literally: a mountain of books)

(*Careful: this system of repeating a *kanji* to obtain a plural only works with a few words.)

page 107

43	23	六十八		16	32	三十三
28	99	二十四		65	41	四十六
56	87	十九		72	17	九十七

page 108–109

Emily: *Juu issai desu.* I'm eleven.
Nico: *Juu ni sai desu.* I'm twelve.
Téo: *Juu ni sai desu. Tanuki-san wa nan sai desu ka.* I'm twelve. How old are you, Tanuki-san?
Tanuki-san: *Ni juu go sai desu.* I'm twenty-five.

page 114

Reading of the letter

Konnichiwa

Namae wa Akira desu. Amerikajin dewa arimasen. Nihonjin no otoko no ko desu. Juu ni sai desu. Chihiro no ani desu. Chihiro wa juu sai no onna no ko desu. Nihon no yama no mura ni sunde imasu. Ie wa inaka ni arimasu. Niwa ga arimasu. Ki to hana ga takusan arimasu. Niwa de watashi to Chihiro wa asobimasu. Kono niwa ga suki desu.

Haha wa kangofu desu. Chichi wa Eigo no sensei desu. Shikashi, watashi wa Eigo o hanashimasen. Watashi no ie ni inu to neko ga imasu. Inu no namae wa Kuro desu. Neko no namae ha Yuki desu. Watashi wa manga to hon ga suki desu. Yama to onsen ga suki desu. Shikashi, umi to machi ga kirai desu. Minasan wa dare desu ka. Doko ni sunde imasuka. Doko no kuni desu ka. Nan sai desu ka. Otoko no ko desu ka. Onna no ko desu ka. Nihongo o hanashimasuka. Nani ga suki desu ka. Nani ga kirai desu ka. Minasan wa watashi no tomodachi ni narimasuka.

Sayonara.

Translation of the letter:

Hello.

My name is Akira. I am not American. I am a Japanese boy. I am twelve years old. I am Chihiro's older brother. Chihiro is a ten-year-old girl.

We live in a mountainous village of Japan. Our house is in the countryside. We have a yard. There are plenty of trees and flowers. My sister and I play in the yard. We like this yard.

Mother is a nurse. Father is an English teacher. But I don't speak English.

In my house, we have a dog and a cat. My dog's name is Kuro. My cat's name is Yuki. I like manga and books. I like the mountains and hot springs. But I don't like oceans and cities.

Who are you guys? Where do you live? In what country? How old are you? Are you boys or girls? Do you speak Japanese? What do you like? What do you dislike? Would you guys become my friends?

Goodbye.

Akira

page 115

1. A boy named Akira.
2. He is Japanese.
3. He is 12.
4. A girl named Chihiro.
5. Yes. Because she's the little sister of the letter's author.
6. She is ten.
7. In a mountainous village of Japan, in the countryside.
8. Yes, there is a yard. There are many trees and flowers in the yard.
9. He plays there with his sister.
10. He talks about his mother and father.
11. The mother is a nurse and the father teaches English.
12. He speaks Japanese (since he's Japanese!). But he does not speak English.
13. Yes, there are animals in his home: a dog and a cat.
14. They are named Kuro and Yuki.
15. They're named that way because of their color. (*kuro* = black; *yuki* = snow = white.)
16. He likes books and manga. He likes mountains and hot springs (*onsen*).
17. He hates the sea and cities.
18. He is addressing Emily, Téo and Nico.
19. He wants to know who they are. Where they live. In what country. How old they are. Whether they're boys or girls. What they like and dislike.
20. He is suggesting they become friends.

Published by Tuttle Publishing, an imprint of Periplus Editions (HK) Ltd.

www.tuttlepublishing.com

English translation copyright © 2010 Periplus Editions (HK) Ltd
© Editions Picquier, 2007
Illustrations © Florence Lérot-Calvo
Phone illustration page 57 nikiteev_konstantin / Shutterstock

Library of Congress Cataloging-in-Publication Data

Galan, Christian.
   I'm learning Japanese! : a language adventure for young people / Christian Galan ; illustrations by Florence Lerot-Calvo. — 1st ed.
       p. cm.
   English and Japanese.
   ISBN 978-4-8053-1074-8
1. Japanese language—Textbooks for Foreign speakers—English—Juvenile literature. 2. Japanese language—Conversation and phrase books—English—Juvenile literature. I. Lerot-Calvo, Florence, ill. II. Title.
   PL539.3.G35 2010
   495.6'82421—dc22
                                    2009045322
ISBN 978-4-8053-1553-8

DISTRIBUTED BY

North America, Latin America & Europe
Tuttle Publishing
364 Innovation Drive
North Clarendon, VT 05759-9436 U.S.A.
Tel: 1 (802) 773-8930; Fax: 1 (802) 773-6993
info@tuttlepublishing.com; www.tuttlepublishing.com

Japan
Tuttle Publishing
Yaekari Building 3rd Floor, 5-4-12 Osaki
Shinagawa-ku, Tokyo 141-0032
Tel: (81) 3 5437-0171; Fax: (81) 3 5437-0755
sales@tuttle.co.jp; www.tuttle.co.jp

Asia Pacific
Berkeley Books Pte. Ltd.
3 Kallang Sector #04-01,
Singapore 349278
Tel: (65) 6741 2178; Fax: (65) 6741 2179
inquiries@periplus.com.sg; www.tuttlepublishing.com

Revised edition
25 24 23 22   10 9 8 7 6 5

Printed in Singapore   2203TP

Books to Span the East and West

Our core mission at Tuttle Publishing is to create books which bring people together one page at a time. Tuttle was founded in 1832 in the small New England town of Rutland, Vermont (USA). Our fundamental values remain as strong today as they were then—to publish best-in-class books informing the English-speaking world about the countries and peoples of Asia. The world is a smaller place today and Asia's economic, cultural and political influence has expanded, yet the need for meaningful dialogue and information about this diverse region has never been greater. Since 1948, Tuttle has been a leader in publishing books on the cultures, arts, cuisines, languages and literatures of Asia. Our authors and photographers have won many awards and Tuttle has published thousands of titles on subjects ranging from martial arts to paper crafts. We welcome you to explore the wealth of information available on Asia at **www.tuttlepublishing.com.**

For Clément and Julien

For Barbara